# how to use this book

## SYMBOLS

- ✉ address
- ☎ telephone number
- ⊖ nearest tube station
- 🚆 nearest train/DLR station
- 🚌 nearest bus route
- ⛴ nearest ferry wharf
- 🕘 opening hours
- ℹ tourist information
- $ cost, entry charge
- [e] email/website address
- ♿ wheelchair access
- 🚸 child-friendly
- 🍴 on-site or nearby eatery
- [V] good vegetarian selection

## COLOUR-CODING

Each chapter has a different colour code which is reflected on the maps for quick reference (eg all Highlights are bright yellow on the maps).

## MAPS

The fold-out maps inside the front and back covers are numbered from 1 to 6. All sights and venues in the text have map references which indicate where to find them on the maps; eg (6, H4) means Map 6, grid reference H4. Although each item is not pin-pointed on the maps, the street address is always indicated.

## PRICES

Price gradings (eg £10/8/7.50/6/30 a/s/st/c/f) indicate adult (a), senior (s), student (st), child (c) and family (f) entry charges to a venue. Most family tickets cover two adults and two children.

## AUTHOR AUTHOR !

**Steve Fallon**

Having fled from the overly fresh air, monotonous greenery and the deafening tranquillity of deepest rural Essex where he 'did time' for four years, Steve Fallon is now luxuriating in the pollution, concrete and general hubbub of London, one of the world's most vibrant and exciting cities. For this book he did everything the hard way: walking the walks, seeing the sights, taking (some) advice from friends, colleagues and the odd taxi driver and digesting everything in sight – right down to that last pint. Says he: 'Thank God I'm a city boy (again).'

## READER FEEDBACK

Things change – prices go up, schedules change, good places go bad and bad places improve or go bankrupt. So, if you find things better or worse, recently opened or long since closed, please tell us and help make the next edition even more accurate. Send all correspondence to the Lonely Planet office closest to you (listed on p. 2) or visit www.lonelyplanet.com/feedback/.

**Lonely Planet books provide independent advice. Lonely Planet does not accept advertising in guidebooks, nor payment in exchange for listing or endorsing any place or business. Lonely Planet writers do not accept discounts or payments in exchange for positive coverage of any sort.**

# LONDON

## CONDENSED

 steve fallon

LONELY PLANET PUBLICATIONS
Melbourne • Oakland • London • Paris

# contents

London Condensed
2nd edition – May 2002
First published – April 2000

Published by
Lonely Planet Publications Pty Ltd
ABN 36 005 607 983
90 Maribyrnong St, Footscray, Vic 3011, Australia
www.lonelyplanet.com or AOL keyword: lp

Lonely Planet offices
Australia Locked Bag 1, Footscray, Vic 3011
        ☎ 613 8379 8000  fax 613 8379 8111
        e talk2us@lonelyplanet.com.au
USA     150 Linden St, Oakland, CA 94607
        ☎ 510 893 8555  Toll Free: 800 275 8555
        fax 510 893 8572
        e info@lonelyplanet.com
UK      10a Spring Place, London NW5 3BH
        ☎ 020 7428 4800  fax 020 7428 4828
        e go@lonelyplanet.co.uk
France  1 rue du Dahomey, 75011 Paris
        ☎ 01 55 25 33 00  fax 01 55 25 33 01
        e bip@lonelyplanet.fr
        www.lonelyplanet.fr

Design Annika Roojun Editing Emma Sangster
Maps Rachel Beattie Cover James Hardy Publishing
Manager Diana Saad Thanks to Abigail Hole, Amanda
Canning, Charles Rawlings-Way, Gabrielle Green,
Heather Dickson, James Ellis, James Hardy, Paul Piaia,
Rowan McKinnon, Ryan Evans

Photographs
Many of the images in this guide are available for
licensing from Lonely Planet Images:
e www.lonelyplanetimages.com

Front cover photographs
Top Tower Bridge
(Manfred Gottschalk)
Bottom The Thames Barrier
(Charlotte Hindle)

ISBN 1 86450 301 7

Text & maps © Lonely Planet Publications Pty Ltd 2002
London Underground map © Transport for London
Photos © photographers as indicated 2002
Printed by The Bookmaker International Ltd
Printed in China

# facts about london

It's no exaggeration to say that London offers visitors more than any other European city. Not only is it home to such familiar landmarks as Big Ben, St Paul's Cathedral, Tower Bridge, the timeless Thames and the ever-present London Eye Ferris wheel, it also boasts some of the world's greatest museums and art galleries and more parkland than most other capitals. And the opportunities for entertainment after dark? From pubs and clubs to theatre and opera, they go on and on and on.

Along with all that, London is the link that unites those who were rocked in the soft cradle of the English language or slept on its comfortable cushions later on. This is both the tongue's birthplace and its epicentre; for many people a visit to London is like a homecoming.

At the same time, London is an amazingly tolerant place, its people pretty much unflappable. Many first-time visitors are surprised to discover how multicultural the British capital is and how well most of the three dozen or so ethnic minorities get along together.

London is not, and never will be, the 'museumland' that is Paris nor a tidy, flower-bedecked Amsterdam; most of its citizens wouldn't have it either way. Both gritty and savant, loud-mouthed and understated, London exhilarates and intimidates, stimulates as well as irritates. It offers different things to different people and so it will you. Breathe deeply in this world-class city and – once your coughing fit subsides – you will have ingested enough history, culture, sleaze, disappointment, joy and kindness to last half a lifetime.

Neil Setchfield

*Pods of people aboard London's eye-catching Ferris wheel: the BA London Eye*

## HISTORY

London was settled by the Romans, and much of the area, particularly the City of London, has since been inhabited continuously. As a result, archaeologists have had to wait for redevelopment to make sites available for excavation. The building boom of the 1980s revealed an astonishing number of finds, and the practice continues; major discoveries are being made annually. For an easy and entertaining run through London's history, visit the Museum of London near the Barbican (see p. 37).

### The Celts & Romans

Although the Celts settled round a ford on the southern bank of the Thames, it was the Romans who first developed the area north of the river in the 1st century AD, calling it Londinium. They built a bridge and an impressive city wall, and made the city an important port and the hub of their road system.

### The Saxons & Danes

The Romans deserted Londinium in AD410, and the Saxons, Teutonic tribes originating from north of the Rhine, established farmsteads and settled in small villages in the area. Few clues of London in the Dark Ages remain, but the town survived the 200-year onslaught by the Danes (or Vikings).

Less than a decade before the Normans arrived from northern France at the end of the 11th century, Edward the Confessor moved his court to a new palace at Westminster and founded an abbey nearby.

### The Normans

After his victory at the Battle of Hastings in 1066, William the Conqueror found himself in control of a city that was by far the largest, richest and most powerful in the Saxon kingdom. The Norman ruler distrusted the 'vast and fierce populace' of London and raised the White Tower, the core of the Tower of London stronghold, but he also confirmed the city's independence and right to self-government.

### A Pox on London

In mid-17th-century London, the shout 'garde loo' alerted passers-by that a chamber pot was about to be emptied into the street from an upstairs window. Crowded, filthy London had suffered from recurrent outbreaks of bubonic plague since the 14th century, but nothing had prepared it for the Great Plague of 1665 in which around 100,000 people died.

### Tudor London

During the reign (1558-1603) of Elizabeth I, daughter of Henry VIII, London began to expand rapidly; in the half-century up to 1600 the population doubled to 200,000. Sadly, medieval, Tudor and Jacobean London was destroyed in a stroke by the Great Fire of 1666. The inferno gave Christopher Wren a clean slate on which to build his famous churches but did nothing to halt, or rein in, the city's growth.

## Georgian Period

By 1700 there were approximately 600,000 Londoners and, as the seat of Parliament and focal point for a growing empire, London was becoming ever richer and more important.

Georgian architects such as John Nash, the planner of Trafalgar Square, and Sir John Soane, who built the Bank of England, replaced the last of medieval London with imposing symmetrical architecture and residential squares.

## Victorian Age

The population exploded in the 19th century, creating a vast expanse of suburbs to the south and east during the 64-year reign of Queen Victoria. Spurred by the Industrial

*The immense, oval Royal Albert Hall*

Revolution and the empire's rapidly expanding trade and commerce, the population of London jumped from just under a million in 1801 (the year of the first national census) to 6.5 million a century later.

## WWII & Postwar

Much of east London was obliterated by the Blitz, and by the time the war ended in 1945, some 32,000 Londoners had been killed and another 50,000 seriously wounded. After the war, ugly housing and low-cost developments were thrown up on the bomb sites. The Thames docks, once an important mainstay of London's economy, never recovered; shipping moved east to Tilbury, and the Docklands declined to the point of dereliction until redevelopment began in the mid-1980s.

## London Today

Riding on a wave of Thatcherite confidence and deregulation, the Conservatives were elected for a fourth successive term in 1992, but

> ### What's in a Name?
> The '-wich' (or '-wych') in names such as Greenwich, Aldwych and Dulwich comes from the Saxon word *wic*, meaning 'settlement'. *Ea* or *ey* is an old word for 'island' or 'marsh'; thus Chelsea (Island of Sand), Bermondsey (Bermond's Island) and Hackney (Haca's Marsh). In Old English, *ceap* meant 'trade' or 'market'; hence Eastcheap, where the plebs shopped in medieval times, while Cheapside was reserved for the royal household. 'Borough' comes from *burg*, Old English for 'fort' or 'town'.

the economy soon went into a tailspin. The May 1997 general election returned a Labour government to power for the first time in 18 years; the capital's booming economy and low unemployment, a feeble and divided opposition and the strong leadership of Prime Minister Tony Blair all contributed to Labour's landslide victory in June 2001.

## ORIENTATION

Greater London encompasses 610 sq miles (1580 sq km) of south-eastern England and is enclosed by the M25 ring road. The Thames is the city's main geographical feature; running from west to east, it flows in wide bends and in its wake creates peninsulas that can make it unclear what side of the river you're on at times.

London is divided into 33 widely differing boroughs (13 of them in central London), which are run by local councils. The 'square mile' (about 2.7 sq km) of the City of London, at the heart of the conurbation, is known simply as 'the City'. The East End is traditionally working class and the London of both Dickens and Hollywood; to the west lies the nightlife centre of Soho. Since Victorian times, boroughs to the west and north have tended to be posher and more affluent than those to the east and south.

### North-South Divide

Although the Thames isn't the physical barrier that it was in the Middle Ages, psychologically the gulf is as wide as ever. Most people in north London (and that's most Londoners) refuse to believe there's anything of importance across the river. A standard question in Londoner-to-Londoner chats is 'When was the last time you crossed the river?' (which usually means 'went south'), and jokes abound about having to get a visa before making the crossing.

## ENVIRONMENT

London's horrendous traffic moves at an average 11 miles/hr (18km/h) – about what it did when horses and coaches clogged the city's narrow streets – and is largely responsible for the city's most serious environmental problem: poor air quality. So bad is the air that most cyclists wear masks to protect themselves from breathing in toxic fumes. The problem could be alleviated by a £5 'congestion charge' levied on every private car entering central London between 7am and 7pm weekdays, which goes into effect in 2003. In any case, those with respiratory problems should heed air-quality forecasts attached to weather bulletins, especially in the warmer months.

To look at the Thames' murky waters you'd assume it was another pollution black spot, but things have improved considerably since efforts to decontaminate the river began in 1974. Today the Thames is home to some 115 species of fish, including shad, sea lamprey and even salmon. With them have come 10,000 herons, cormorants and other waterfowl, which feed on the fish; even otters have been spotted on the river's upper reaches.

*Tour boats on the River Thames, now one of the world's cleanest metropolitan rivers*

Dennis Johnson

## GOVERNMENT & POLITICS

In May 2000, London lost the dubious distinction of being the world's only capital city without a self-governing authority and mayor when independent Ken Livingstone, the former head of the erstwhile Greater London Council (GLC), was elected by popular vote to lead the new Greater London Authority (GLA), the city's regional government. The 25-member London Assembly, with certain authority over transport, economic development, strategic planning, the environment, the police, fire brigades, civil defence and cultural matters, is elected from newly created GLA constituencies (14 members) and by London as a whole (11 members).

The City of London is governed from Guildhall by the Corporation of London, headed by the Lord Mayor and an assortment of oddly named (and even more oddly dressed) aldermen, beadles and sheriffs. These men – and they usually *are* male – are elected by the City of London's freemen and liverymen.

### Livery Companies

In the Middle Ages, most craftsworkers belonged to guilds, prototypes of trade unions. The wealthier ones built themselves magnificent guildhalls, and their leaders, who wore fine costumes, or liveries, were eligible to stand for the chain of offices that culminated in Lord Mayor of the City of London. More than 100 livery companies live on, and their leading lights still stand for office at the Court of Common Council, which runs the Corporation of London.

If you would like to visit one of the guildhalls, contact the Corporation of London's Tourist Information Centre (☎ 7332 1456, e www.city oflondon.gov.uk).

## ECONOMY

Europe's richest city (central London's GDP per head is twice that of Paris) continues to be the driving force behind the British economy, but you'll see few signs of heavy industry here. It is one of the world's major financial centres, with a flourishing service sector employing about half of the workforce; tourism is one of the three most successful industries. Economic indicators continue to be upbeat, with unemployment and inflation levels low and falling, and the city in the midst of a property boom.

Neil Setchfield

### London by Numbers

| | |
|---|---:|
| Central London pop. | 7 million |
| Greater London pop. | 12 million |
| Central London GDP/head | £18,500 |
| London's share of UK GDP | 16% |
| Average house price | £165,400 |
| Annual overseas visitors | 13.2 million |
| Av. visitor expenditure/day | £75 |
| Inflation | 2.5% |
| Unemployment | 6.4% |

# SOCIETY & CULTURE

The most common preconceptions about Londoners – reserved, inhibited and stiflingly polite – are not far off the mark, with passengers travelling in eye-averted silence on the tube and trains. But as London is among the planet's most crowded places, such behaviour is partly a protective veneer, essential for coping with the constant crush of people.

Londoners rise to the fore in a crisis; fall down or have your wallet pinched and the crowds will descend, offering advice, solace and calling the police or an ambulance. In general Londoners are a tolerant bunch, unfazed by outrageous dress or behaviour. Indeed, they are whizzes at ignoring anyone who is trying to draw attention to themselves.

In general, this means relatively low levels of chauvinism, racism, sexism or any other 'ism' you can think of. As Londoners like to say: 'As long as you don't scare the horses, mate, you'll be all right here'.

### Ethnic London

London has a long tradition of attracting (if not always welcoming) refugees from abroad ever since the late 17th century, when Huguenots arrived from France to escape religious persecution. Today, just under 25% of all Londoners are from 33 sizeable (ie, more than 10,000) ethnic communities.

## Dos & Don'ts

It's not especially easy to cause offence in London – unless you're trying to. But try starting a general conversation at a bus stop or on a tube platform and you'll find people reacting as if you were mad; most Londoners would no more speak to a stranger in the street than fly to the moon. If you're obviously a tourist in need of directions, however, there won't be a problem.

**Dress** London is very free and easy about what you wear, but it pays to be respectful in places of religion. A few posh restaurants and many clubs operate strict dress codes. In the former, that usually means a jacket and tie for men, and no jeans or trainers for anyone; in the latter, it means whatever the management and their bouncers choose it to mean on that particular night.

**Queuing** The British have always been addicted to queuing, and the order of the queue at banks, post offices, newsagents etc is sacrosanct – few things are more calculated to spark an outburst of tongue-clucking than an attempt to 'push in' to a line of people. Oh, and please have your money ready.

**The Underground** The tube has its own etiquette. On escalators, you *must* stand on the right so that people can rush up or down on the left. On platforms, move away from the entrance to prevent crowds blocking doorways, which could cause someone to fall onto the rails. When a train pulls in, stand aside until everybody inside has left the carriage. It's considered a 'nicety' – even a social service – to leave behind a newspaper in the morning. In the evening, it's plain trash.

# ARTS

London has a flourishing cultural life. It doesn't matter whether you're talking about art as it is found in the National Gallery, classical concerts at Wigmore Hall or live gigs at music pubs, London still manages to cream off the best.

## Painting

Although London is home to many astounding art collections, British painters have never dominated any particular epoch or style in the way that other European nations have. The early-19th-century Romantic landscape painter JMW Turner is arguably the only British artist who can be counted among the all-time greats of the international art world, though this is not to discount the works of artists such as Thomas Gainsborough, William Hogarth, John Constable, Francis Bacon, Lucian Freud and, more recently, Damien Hirst, Rachel Whiteread and Tracey Emin, of course. Rivalled only by New York, London's gallery scene is as vibrant as ever.

## Literature

The contribution that London and Londoners have made (and continue to make) to the written word is epic. English literature is peppered with writers for whom London provided inspiration: Chaucer, Shakespeare, Dickens, Conan Doyle, HG Wells, Iris Murdoch, Doris Lessing, Hanif Kureishi, Martin Amis, Will Self and Zadie Smith, to name but a few.

### Wren's Churches

The greatest architect ever to leave his mark on London – thus far – was Sir Christopher Wren (1632-1723). After the Great Fire of 1666 had destroyed 88 of the city's churches, Wren was commissioned to rebuild 51 of them, as well as to create a new St Paul's Cathedral (see p. 26). The money for the work was raised by putting a tax on all the coal imported through the Port of London.

Perhaps the most striking features of Wren's new designs were the graceful Renaissance steeples that were to take the place of the solid square towers of the previous medieval churches. Wren went on to build another three churches in London, but some 19 of his churches have been destroyed since 1781. Visit **e** www.london-city-churches.org for more information.

*The soaring spire of Wren's St Bride's Church, Fleet Street*

Simon Bracken

## Music

London is passionate about classical music, with five symphony orchestras, but the city is best known for the popular music waves that have washed over it: from the swinging 60s of the Beatles, Rolling Stones and Kinks to the current quintessentially English indie pop bands such as Oasis, Suede, Pulp and Blur, via 70s glam and prog rock, punk and ska, 80s popsters, 90s girl and boy bands and today's garage. Whatever your musical taste, you will be spoiled for choice.

### Of Rakes & Harlots

William Hogarth (1697-1764) was an artist and engraver who specialised in satire, and his moralising engravings offer an invaluable look at life among the lowly in Georgian London. His eight-plate series *A Harlot's Progress* traces the life of a country lass from her arrival in London to convicted whore. In *A Rake's Progress*, the debauched protagonist is seen being entertained in a Russell St tavern by a bevy of prostitutes, one of whom strokes his chest while the other relieves him of his pocket watch.

Hogarth's works can be seen in Sir John Soane's Museum (see p. 27), Tate Britain (see p. 29) and the National Gallery (see p. 23).

## Theatre

A long tradition in theatre, and healthy support in recent times, via National Lottery proceeds, of ballet, opera and classical music, continues to provide a fertile, if not always creative, environment. With or without music, London's theatre life is lively and remains top billing for visitors. While plays and performances don't always have the wit of Coward or Wilde, the depth of Pinter or the sheer spectacle of the best of Andrew Lloyd Webber, the West End is full of options, and tickets are affordable and easy to come by.

*London's principal theatre for opera and ballet: the Royal Opera House, Covent Garden*

# highlights

Even more than most capital cities, London abounds with things to see and do. Fortunately most of the major sights are clustered together, either in the City of London, the West End, Bloomsbury or Westminster.

The museums, galleries, palaces, churches, gardens and other attractions listed here are London's top sights; you can't really say you've been to the British capital without having visited at least some of them. That's not to say that these are the only sights in town (see pp. 34-47).

Some sights (eg, the Tower of London and the British Museum) can get very crowded, particularly in summer. Avoid long queues by visiting early in the morning or late in the afternoon and by buying tickets in advance from a tourist information centre (TIC) or some Underground stations.

## Times & Charges

Hours listed in all chapters are *literally* the opening and closing times. Last ad-mission to most venues is at least 30mins before closing time.

Most of London's finest museums and galleries are now free to all, but funding remains a problem. There are donation boxes (£2 requested) at the entrances to most. Special exhibits may incur a separate entrance fee.

Keen sightseers should check out the London Pass, which allows free ad-mission to over 50 museums and other attractions. See page 116 for details.

## Stopping Over?

Try this top-sight itinerary if time is tight:

**One Day** Visit Westminster Abbey and view the Houses of Parliament and Big Ben. Walk up Whitehall, passing Downing St, the Cenotaph and Horse Guards Parade. Cross Trafalgar Square to visit the National Gallery. Walk to Piccadilly Circus to see the statue of Eros.

**Two Days** Visit the British Museum and walk west along Oxford St and up Baker St to Madame Tussaud's.

**Three Days** Visit one of South Kensington's museums (the Victoria & Albert, Natural History or Science). Kensington Palace is only a short distance to the northwest. Alternatively, go up Brompton Rd towards Hyde Park Corner and walk along Constitution Hill to take in the view of Buckingham Palace.

## Lowlights

Some of the things we could do without (or at least with less of):

- 11pm pub closings – still!
- most of the Underground and its horrendous service
- soulless Leicester Square
- hellishly cacophonous London Trocadero
- London Dungeon
- bad signposting on several streets
- poor value for money in many restaurants
- scurrilous tabloid newspapers
- Heathrow Airport

## BRITISH AIRWAYS LONDON EYE (3, H8)

At the south-western corner of riverside **Jubilee Gardens**, the site of the 1951 Festival of Britain and now being extended northwards as far as Hungerford Bridge, is the colossal British Airways (BA) London Eye (aka the **Millennium Wheel**). At 135m tall, it is the world's largest Ferris wheel and London's fourth tallest structure. It's a thrilling experience to sit in one of the 32 enclosed glass gondolas, enjoying views of some 25 miles (40km) on clear days across the capital, and particularly so for Londoners; most tall buildings in the city are closed to the public and this is about as high as most locals will ever get in their home town. The Millennium Wheel takes a full 30 minutes to rotate completely and each capsule holds 25 passengers.

Like many other public works projects here, the wheel went through a series of teething problems at the start, and original plans were for the wheel to remain on site until 2005 and then be moved elsewhere. But since opening in 2000, the public's reaction has been overwhelmingly in favour of the wheel and most Londoners love it. Most importantly, it's turned into something of a city icon. The BA London Eye looks like it's here to stay.

### INFORMATION

✉ Jubilee Gardens SE1
☎ 0870 500 0600
[e] www.ba-londoneye.com
⊖ Waterloo
🕘 Jan-Apr & Oct-Dec: 9.30am-8pm; May-Sept: 9.30am-10pm
$ £8.50/6.50/5 a/s/c Jan-Mar; £9/7/5 Apr-June & Oct-Dec; £9.50/7.50/5 Jul-Sept
♿ excellent
🍴 Gourmet Pizza Company

Neil Setchfield

Neil Setchfield

*High in the sky on the London Eye*

### London's Bridges

London counts 15 bridges between the neo-Gothic Tower Bridge in the east and Battersea Bridge in the south-west. The one with the longest history is London Bridge linking Southwark and the City. The most beautiful is the ill-fated Millennium Bridge between Bankside and the City, which had to close for 1½ years due to safety concerns immediately after it opened in June 2000. The newest is Jubilee Bridge built onto an existing walkway alongside Cannon Street railway bridge and set to open in late 2002. It is London's first covered bridge since the original London Bridge went up in 1176.

# BRITISH MUSEUM    (3, D6)

This is the UK's largest museum, one of the oldest in the world and the most visited tourist attraction in London (with some 5.7 million visitors per year).

As part of the millennium celebrations, the museum underwent a major renovation and the inner courtyard, hidden from the public for almost a century and a half, was covered with a spectacular glass and steel roof and is now the light-filled **Great Court**. In the heart of the Great Court is the **Reading Room**, where George Bernard Shaw and Mahatma Gandhi studied and Karl Marx wrote *The Communist Manifesto*.

The collections inside originated with the curiosities collected by the physician Hans Sloane (of Sloane Square fame), sold to the nation in 1753 and augmented not long afterwards with manuscripts and books from the two other major collections.

The museum is vast, diverse and exceedingly rich – so much so that it can seem pretty daunting. To make the most of the museum don't plan on seeing too much in one day; remember, admission is free so you can come back several times to appreciate the exhibits at your leisure.

The back entrance off Montague Place tends to be less congested than the imposing porticoed main one off Great Russell St. Whether you take a tour or use the plan of the museum to find your own way round, the most obvious strategy is to home straight in on the highlights, but bear in mind that most people will be doing the same thing.

Simon Bracken

Neil Setchfield

*The British Museum Great Court*

**INFORMATION**

- ✉ Great Russell St WC1
- ☎ 7636 1555, 7323 8000
- e www.thebritish museum.ac.uk
- ⊖ Tottenham Court Road, Russell Square
- ◷ Sat-Wed 10am-5.30pm, Thurs & Fri 10am-8.30pm
- $ free, £2 donation suggested
- ① Highlights audio-guide £3.50 (90mins); Highlights tour £8/5 a/c&st (90mins); free eyeOpeners 11-3pm (50-60mins)
- ♿ good; ☎ 7637 7384; free booklet available
- ✗ Court Cafe, Gallery Cafe, Court Restaurant

**DON'T MISS**
- Egyptian Mummies ● Elgin Marbles ● Oxus Treasure
- Rosetta Stone ● Sutton Hoo Treasure

# BUCKINGHAM PALACE (3, J4)

Buckingham Palace, built as Buckingham House in 1705 for the duke of Buckingham, has been the royal family's London home since 1837 when St James's Palace was judged too old fashioned and insufficiently impressive. A total of 19 staterooms (out of 661) are open to visitors in August and September, but don't expect to see the Queen's bedroom. She and the duke of Edinburgh share a strictly off-limits suite of 12 rooms overlooking Green Park.

**INFORMATION**

✉ The Mall SW1
☎ 7839 1377 or 7321 2233 (advance bookings)
[e] www.the-royal-collection.org.uk
⊖ St James's Park, Victoria
🕒 Aug-Sept 9.30am-4.30pm
$ £11/9/5.50/27.50 a/s/c/f
[i] changing of the guard Apr-Aug 11.30am, Sept-Mar alternate days (☎ 09068 6633 44 for exact dates)
♿ good
🍴 ICA Cafe

Neil Setchfield

The tour begins in the **Guard Room** and includes a peek at the **State Dining Room** (all red damask and Regency furnishings, with a portrait of George III looking rather fetching in fur); **Queen Victoria's Picture Gallery** (a full 76.5m long, with works by Rembrandt, Van Dyck, Canaletto, Poussin and Vermeer); the **Blue Drawing Room**, with a gorgeous fluted ceiling by John Nash; the **White Drawing Room**, where the monarch receives ambassadors accredited to the Court of St James; and the **Ballroom**, where official receptions and state banquets are held. Visitors get the biggest kick out of seeing the **Throne Room**, with his-and-hers pink chairs with the initials 'ER' and 'P' sitting smugly under what looks like a theatre arch.

The **changing of the guard**, when the old guard comes off duty to be replaced by the new, is one of those quintessential English events. Taking place on the forecourt of Buckingham Palace, tourists have a chance to gape at the guards' bright red uniforms and bearskin hats. If you arrive early, grab a spot by the railings; more likely, however, you'll be 10 rows back and hardly able to see a thing.

## Victoria Memorial

While you're waiting for the guard to change, take a peek at the Queen Victoria Memorial (1911) in the middle of the roundabout. Carved from a single block of white marble and almost 25m high, it portrays Victoria – an intelligent, progressive and passionate woman despite the bad rap she gets in the history books – surrounded by a number of allegorical figures representing everything from Charity and Justice to Painting and Progress.

Neil Setchfield

# COURTAULD GALLERY (3, F8)

Housed in the North Wing (or Strand Block) of the splendid Palladian **Somerset House** (1775), the gallery displays some of the Courtauld Institute of Art's marvellous collection of paintings in grand surrounds following a £25 million architectural refurbishment. Exhibits include works by Rubens, Velásquez and Botticelli but for many visitors the most memorable display is the impressionist and postimpressionist art by Van Gogh, Cézanne, Manet, Pissarro, Sisley, Henri Rousseau, Toulouse-Lautrec, Degas, Gauguin, Renoir and Monet shown on the top floor.

The gallery also has a small exhibition of paintings by the 20th-century Bloomsbury artists Duncan Grant, Vanessa Bell and Roger Fry, together with colourful furniture produced by the Omega Workshops (also in Bloomsbury) and influenced by what were then newly discovered African masks and other ethnographical items.

Somerset House, whose central **Great Court** was once a car park for civil servants and is now a gauntlet of 55 dancing fountains and an ice-skating rink in winter, is home to two other notable collections: the incredibly rich **Gilbert Collection** of European silver, gold snuff boxes and Italian mosaics, and the **Hermitage Rooms**, with rotating exhibits on loan from the State Hermitage Museum in St Petersburg. Opening hours and fees are similar to those at the Courtauld.

Neil Setchfield

Neil Setchfield

*The 18th-century Somerset House*

## INFORMATION

- ✉ Somerset House, The Strand WC2
- ☎ 7848 2526
- e www.courtauld.ac.uk
- ↔ Temple (closed Sun), Embankment
- ⏱ mid-Apr–Aug: 10am-6pm (late July-early Sept: Fri 10am-9pm); Sept–mid-Apr: Mon-Sat 10am-6pm, Sun 12-6pm
- 💲 £4/3 a/s&st; free Mon 10am-2pm; joint Courtauld Gallery/Gilbert Collection ticket £7.50/5/6 a/s/st
- ⓘ 1hr guided tours Tues, Thurs & Sat 12pm, £5.50
- ♿ excellent
- ✗ Coffee Gallery

**DON'T MISS**
- Botticelli's *The Trinity* • Manet's *Le Déjeuner sur l'Herbe*
- Modigliani's *Female Nude* • Rubens' *Moonlight Landscape*
- Van Gogh's *Self-Portrait with Bandaged Ear*

## HOUSES OF PARLIAMENT (3, J7)

The Houses of Parliament (ie, the House of Commons and the House of Lords) are in what is known as the Palace of Westminster, built by Charles Barry and Augustus Pugin in 1840 when the neo-Gothic style was all the rage. The most famous feature outside the palace is the Clock Tower, commonly known as **Big Ben** (the real Ben, a bell named after Benjamin Hall, the commissioner of works when the tower was completed in 1858, hangs inside). At the opposite end of the building is Victoria Tower (1860).

The **House of Commons** is where Parliament meets to propose and discuss new legislation, apart from a three-month summer recess and Easter and Christmas breaks. Expect long queues to visit the Strangers' Gallery where one can see the Commons at work. You shouldn't have any trouble getting into the visitors' gallery of the **House of Lords**.

Left of the security area is the stunning hammer-beam roof of **Westminster Hall**. Originally built in 1099, it is the oldest surviving part of the Palace of Westminster, the seat of English monarchy from the 11th to the early 16th centuries. Added between 1394 and 1401, the roof has been described as 'the greatest surviving achievement of medieval English carpentry'. Westminster Hall served in part as a courthouse until the 19th century and the trials of William Wallace (1305), Sir Thomas More (1535), Guy Fawkes (1606) and Charles I (1649) all took place here. More recently it was used for the lying-in-state of Sir Winston Churchill in 1965.

### INFORMATION

✉ Parliament Sq SW1 (visitors: St Stephen's Entrance, St Margaret St SW1)
☎ 7219 4272 (House of Commons Visitors' Gallery), 7219 3107 (House of Lords Visitors' Gallery)
[e] www.parliament.uk
⊖ Westminster
🕘 when Parliament is sitting – Commons Mon-Wed 2.30-10.30pm, Thurs 11.30am-7.30pm, Fri 9.30am-3pm; Lords Mon-Wed 2.30-7.30pm, Thurs 3-7.30pm, Fri 11am-3pm
$ free
ℹ guided tours (☎ 7344 9966) early Aug-late Sept Mon-Sat 9.15am-4.30pm, £3.50
♿ good
🍴 Westminster Arms

Neil Setchfield

### House of Commons

Based on St Stephen's Chapel in the original Palace of Westminster, the current chamber, designed by Giles Gilbert Scott, replaced an earlier version destroyed in 1941. Although the Commons is a national assembly of 659 Members of Parliament (MPs), the chamber only seats 437. Government members sit to the right of the Speaker; the Opposition to the left. The House Speaker presides over business from a chair given by Australia; ministers speak from a despatch box donated by New Zealand.

# IMPERIAL WAR MUSEUM (3, K10)

The Imperial War Museum is housed in a striking building dating from 1815 and crowned with a magnificent copper dome in 1845. This was originally the site of the Bethlehem Royal Hospital, commonly known as Bedlam, an infirmary for the insane.

Although there's still plenty of military hardware on show and the core of the six-floor museum is a chronological exhibition on the two world wars, these days the museum places more emphasis on the social cost of war: the Blitz, the food shortages, the propaganda. The 2nd floor features war paintings by the likes of Stanley Spencer and John Singer Sargent.

Particularly popular exhibits are the **Trench Experience**, which depicts the grim day-to-day existence of a WWI infantryman in a frontline trench on the Somme, and the **Blitz Experience**, which lets visitors sit inside a mock bomb-shelter during an air raid and then stroll through ravaged East End streets. Both are on the lower-ground floor. Another popular one is the **Secret War Exhibition** on the 1st floor, which takes a look at the work of the secret services from 1909 to the present day. The museum's biggest draw, however, is the **Holocaust Exhibition**, which opened in summer 2000 on the 3rd floor.

Charlotte Hindle

**INFORMATION**

- ✉ Lambeth Rd SE1
- ☎ 7416 5320, 0891 600140
- [e] www.iwm.org.uk
- ⊖ Lambeth North
- 🕐 10am-6pm
- $ free
- ⓘ visit early morning or late afternoon to avoid school groups
- ♿ excellent
- 🍴 The Café

Neil Setchfield

*In the wars at the Imperial War Museum*

**DON'T MISS**
- Art galleries • Enigma encrypting machine • V2 Rocket
- Tibetan Peace Garden • Berlin wall fragment

# KENSINGTON PALACE                    (2, G4)

Sometime home to Princess Margaret and the residence of the late Diana, princess of Wales, after her divorce from Prince Charles in 1986, Kensington Palace dates from 1605.

## INFORMATION

✉ Kensington Palace State Apartments W8

☎ 7937 9561

e www.hrp.org.uk

⊖ Queensway, Notting Hill Gate

🕐 palace Mar-Oct 10am-5pm, Nov-Feb 10am-4pm; park & gardens 5am-30mins before dusk

$ palace £8.80/6.90/6.30/26.80 a/s&st/c/f; park & gardens free

ⓘ tours are self-paced & via audioguide (about 1½ hrs)

♿ good

✗ Orangery (p. 82)

Neil Setchfield

Simon Bracken

*The south front of Kensington Palace*

In 1688, William and Mary of Orange bought the house and had it adapted by Sir Christopher Wren and Nicholas Hawksmoor. When George I arrived from Hanover to succeed Queen Anne, he recruited William Kent to modernise the palace. Much of the existing decor is a mix of the small, wood-panelled Stuart State Apartments and Kent's grander, although sometimes clumsy, renovation. Queen Victoria was born here in 1819.

Displayed under low lights are costumes from the **Royal Ceremonial Dress Collection**, including dresses with skirts so ludicrously wide that they made it impossible for their wearers to sit down, ensuring that rooms were sparsely furnished, lest tables and chairs be knocked over. The major draw here, though, is a striking collection of frocks worn by Diana, princess of Wales.

Most beautiful of all the rooms is the **Cupola Room** where the ceremony of initiating men into the exclusive Order of the Garter took place. The order's crest is painted in all its finery on the trompe l'oeil domed ceiling, and the room is ringed with marbled columns and niches in which gilded Roman statues stand.

The **Sunken Garden** near the palace is at its prettiest in summer. Nearby is the **Orangery**, designed by Hawksmoor and Vanbrugh with carvings by Grinling Gibbons, and now a tearoom.

**DON'T MISS**
- Kent's two-eyed Cyclops (King's Long Gallery) • King's Staircase
- Queen Victoria Memorial Room • Round Pond • Van Dyck's *Cupid and Venus* (King's Drawing Room)

# KEW GARDENS (1, B4)

One of the most popular attractions on the London tourist itinerary, the Royal Botanic Gardens at Kew can get very crowded during summer. Spring is probably the best time to visit, but at any time of year this 120-hectare expanse of lawns, formal gardens and greenhouses has delights to offer.

Wonderful plants and trees aside, there are several specific sights within the gardens, such as the metal-and-glass **Palm House** (1848), designed by Decimus Burton and Richard Turner, which houses all sorts of exotic tropical greenery. To the north-west is the tiny but irresistible **Water Lily House** (open Mar-Dec only) and the **Princess of Wales Conservatory**, housing plants in 10 different computer-controlled climate zones. Beyond that is the **Kew Gardens Gallery**, with exhibitions of paintings and photos on a broadly botanical theme.

Set in especially pretty gardens and closed for extensive renovations is the red-brick **Kew Palace** (1631), once a royal residence and very popular with George III whose wife Charlotte died here in 1818. To the south-west you will find **Queen Charlotte's Cottage**, a wooden summerhouse used by the same monarch and his family and surrounded by bluebells in spring.

Among other highlights are the **Japanese Gateway**, the celebrated **Great Pagoda**, designed by William Chambers in 1761, and the **Marianne North Gallery**, featuring the botanical paintings of the indefatigable Victorian female traveller North, who roamed the globe from 1871 to 1885.

Neil Setchfield

## INFORMATION

✉ Kew Rd, Kew, Surrey
☎ 8332 5000, 8940 1171
[e] www.rbgkew.org.uk
⊖ Kew Gardens
⛴ from Westminster Pier (1½hrs) up to 5/day late Mar-Sept/Oct (£7/11 single/return) ☎ 7930 4721
🕘 gardens 9.30am-dusk; glasshouses Mar-Oct 9.30am-5.30pm, Nov-Feb 9.30am-4.15pm
$ £6.50/4.50 a/s&st; late admission (45mins before hothouses close) £4.50
ⓘ Kew Explorer hop-on, hop-off minitrain (£2.50), which circles the gardens in 30mins
♿ good
🍴 Orangery restaurant

### Kew's Serious Side

As well as being a public garden and park, Kew is an important scientific research centre and can claim the most exhaustive botanical collection in the world. Its primary concern is the accurate identification of plants from around the world, but it also is involved in the conservation of endangered plants species and acts as a quarantine station.

# MADAME TUSSAUD'S (3, C2)

Madame Tussaud's is the fourth most popular sight in London (after the British Museum, Tate Modern and National Gallery), with some 2.7 million visitors annually.

Much of the modern Madame Tussaud's is made up of the **Garden Party** exhibition at the start, where you can have your picture taken alongside celebrities – from Pierce Brosnan and Hugh Grant to Whoopi Goldberg and Kylie Minogue. The **Grand Hall** is where you'll find models of world leaders past and present, of the royal family (minus Sarah 'Fergie' Ferguson, the errant duchess of York, and with a dead-ringer model of Diana, princess of Wales, on the sidelines) and of pop stars such as The Beatles. And what happens to those whose 15 minutes of fame has come and gone? Their heads are removed as surely as Marie Antoinette's was and stored in a cupboard – just in case they get another stab at it. In the **Spirit of London** 'time taxi', you sit in a mock-up of a London black cab and are whipped through a five-minute summary of London's history.

### INFORMATION

✉ Marylebone Rd NW1
☎ 0870 400 3000
[e] www.madame-tussauds.com
⊖ Baker Street
🕘 June–mid-Sept: 9am-5.30pm; mid-Sept–May: Mon-Fri 10am-5.30pm, Sat-Sun 9.30am-5.30pm
$ £12/9.50/8.50 a/s/c (£14.45/11.30/10 with Planetarium)
♿ good
🍴 Cafe Tussaud's

Simon Bracken

The **Chamber of Horrors** has models of contemporary prisoners sitting uneasily alongside representations of historic horrors including the mutilated corpse of one of Jack the Ripper's victims. But it all seems somewhat tame after the London Dungeon's blood-fest.

Attached to Madame Tussaud's, the **London Planetarium** presents 30-minute spectaculars on the stars and planets livened up with special effects.

### Madame Wax

Madame Tussaud's – or Madame Tussaud's Waxworks as it was once known – dates back to 1835 when the eponymous Frenchwoman set up her museum with 35 figures, many of them those of people guillotined during the French Revolution. The **200 Years** exhibition shows Madame T herself working on a death mask from the head of Marie Antoinette in her original studio.

Simon Bracken

## NATIONAL GALLERY (6, D6)

The porticoed facade of the National Gallery extends along the northern side of the square. Founded in 1824 and counting more than 2000 European paintings on display at any one time, it's one of the world's largest – and richest – art galleries. The lovely **Sainsbury Wing** on the western side was only added after considerable controversy; Prince Charles, not known for his cutting-edge sense of architectural design, dismissed one proposal as 'a carbuncle on the face of a much loved friend'. Outside the gallery – rather incongruously in this, the heart of London – is a **statue of George Washington**, the man who 'robbed' England of its colonies in the New World. The statue was donated by the Commonwealth of Virginia in 1921.

The paintings in the National Gallery are hung in a continuous time-line; by starting in the Sainsbury Wing and progressing eastwards you can take in a collection of pictures painted between the mid-13th and early 20th centuries in chronological order. If you're keen on the real oldies (1260-1510), head for the Sainsbury Wing; for the Renaissance (1510-1600), go to the **West Wing** in the main building. Rubens, Rembrandt and Caravaggio are in the **North Wing** (1600-1700); if you're after Gainsborough, Constable, Turner, Hogarth and the French Impressionists visit the **East Wing** (1700-1900). For a larger collection of British paintings visit the **Tate Britain** at Millbank (p. 29); for paintings dating after 1900, go to the **Tate Modern** in Bankside (p. 30).

Neil Setchfield

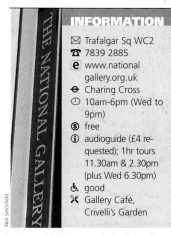

**INFORMATION**

- ✉ Trafalgar Sq WC2
- ☎ 7839 2885
- [e] www.nationalgallery.org.uk
- ⊖ Charing Cross
- 🕘 10am-6pm (Wed to 9pm)
- $ free
- ⓘ audioguide (£4 requested); 1hr tours 11.30am & 2.30pm (plus Wed 6.30pm)
- ♿ good
- 🍴 Gallery Café, Crivelli's Garden

Neil Setchfield

*The National Gallery's impressive main (eastern) portico*

**DON'T MISS**

• Da Vinci's *The Leonardo Cartoon* • Turner's *The Fighting Temeraire* • Van Gogh's *Sunflowers* • Velásquez's *The Rokeby Venus* • *The Wilton Diptych*

# NATIONAL MARITIME MUSEUM (5, D3)

While this museum is a highly recommended destination in its own right, it is also a good excuse to visit Greenwich, which is quaint, village-like and packed with splendid architecture. Its strong connections with the sea, science, sovereigns and – of course – time helped to put it on UNESCO's list of World Heritage Sites (as Maritime Greenwich) in 1997.

The National Maritime Museum, a massive collection of boats, maps, charts, uniforms and marine art, sets out and succeeds in telling the long and convoluted history of Britain as a seafaring nation.

As part of the millennium celebrations, the museum's central

courtyard, **Neptune Court**, was covered with a huge single-span glass roof to provide easy access to some 20 themed galleries on two of the museum's three levels. The galleries have interactive displays and video art that focus on such things as marine ecology and the future of the sea, the tea trade and slavery, and art and the sea.

Videos in the **Nelson Gallery** on the 3rd level tell the story of the battles of the Nile and Trafalgar, and there's an impressive display of Nelson memorabilia, including his tunic with a hole from the bullet that killed him and the actual bullet itself. **All Hands** is an on-board interactive display for children on gunnery, signalling and deep-sea diving.

Attached to the National Maritime Museum is the Palladian **Queen's House**, a Palladian originally deigned by Inigo Jones and once home to Charles I and his queen, Henrietta Maria. Exhibits here focus on illustrious seafarers and historic Greenwich.

## The Longitude Link

Establishing accurate longitude had stumped astronomers from the Greeks to Galileo and as British overseas trade expanded mistakes were costing time, money and lives. When the Royal Observatory (p. 39) successfully tested John Harrison's marine chronometer in 1762, Greenwich had made its place on the map (and the clock). In 1884 the imaginary line passing through the observatory was declared 'the initial meridian for longitude'; Greenwich Mean Time (GMT) has been accepted as the universal measurement of standard time ever since.

Juliet Coombe

*View from the Royal Observatory*

# NATURAL HISTORY MUSEUM (2, H5)

The Natural History Museum now incorporates two collections: the adjoining Life Galleries (entrance on Cromwell Rd) and Earth Galleries (enter from Exhibition Rd). Where once the **Life Galleries** were full of dusty glass cases of butterflies and stick insects, you'll now find wonderful interactive displays on themes such as **Human Biology** and **Creepy Crawlies**, alongside the crowd-attracting exhibition on mammals and dinosaurs, which include animatronic movers and shakers such as the 4m-high **Tyrannosaurus rex**.

In some ways, though, it's the **Earth Galleries** that are the most staggering with an escalator that slithers up and through a hollowed-out globe. Around its base, fine samples of different rocks and gems are beautifully displayed.

Upstairs there are two main exhibits: **Earthquake** and the **Restless Surface**, which explains how wind, water, ice, gravity and life itself impact on the earth. Earthquake is an extraordinary moving and shaking mock-up of what happened to a small grocery shop during the 1995 Kobe trembler in Japan that killed 6000 people. Excellent exhibitions on lower floors include **Earth Today & Tomorrow**, which focuses on ecology, and **From the Beginning**, which explores how planets are formed.

The museum is housed in one of London's finest Gothic Revival buildings. Designed by Alfred Waterhouse between 1873 and 1880 it has a grand cathedral-like main entrance, a gleaming blue and Rsand-coloured brick and terracotta frontage, thin columns and articulated arches, and carvings of plants and animals crawling all over it.

Neil Setchfield

**INFORMATION**

- ✉ Cromwell Rd SW7
- ☎ 7942 5000
- [e] www.nhm.ac.uk
- ⊖ South Kensington
- 🕘 Mon-Sat 10am-5.50pm, Sun 11am-5.50pm
- $ free
- [i] visit early morning or late afternoon to avoid school groups
- ♿ excellent
- 🍴 Waterhouse Cafe

Neil Setchfield

*A grand Gothic-style entrance*

**DON'T MISS**

• Blue whale exhibit • Diplodocus dinosaur skeleton • Ecology Gallery's replica rainforest • Minerals and gemstones in the Earth's Treasury • Wildlife Garden

## ST PAUL'S CATHEDRAL (3, E11)

St Paul's Cathedral was built by Sir Christopher Wren between 1675 and 1710 after the Great Fire of London destroyed the medieval cathedral standing on the site. A niche in the Crypt exhibits Wren's plans and his actual working model. The **dome** still dominates the City and is only exceeded in size by St Peter's in Rome.

The floor below the dome is decorated in a compass design and bears Wren's epitaph in Latin: *Lector, si monumentum requiris, circumspice* (Reader, if you seek his monument, look around you). Above the dome are the **Whispering**, **Stone and Golden Galleries**, all reached by a 530-step staircase. It's worth climbing at least as far as the Stone Gallery (378 steps) for a fantastic view of London.

In the cathedral itself are ornately **carved choir stalls** by Grinling Gibbons, **iron gates** by Jean Tijou, and Holman Hunt's *The Light of the World*; notice how the door in the painting opens outwards only and give it some thought. Walk around the altar, with its massive gilded oak canopy, to the **American Chapel**, a memorial to the 28,000 Americans based in Britain who lost their lives during WWII.

### INFORMATION

✉ St Paul's Churchyard EC4
☎ 7236 4128
[e] www.stpauls.co.uk
⊖ St Paul's
🕐 Mon-Sat 8.30am-5pm, evensong most weekdays at 5pm, Sun 3.15pm
$ £5/4/2.50 a/s&st/c
ⓘ 45min audioguide (£3.50/3 a/s&st); 90min guided tours (£2.50/2/1 a/s&st/c) 4 daily
♿ good
🍴 Crypt Café, Refectory restaurant

Neil Setchfield

Neil Setchfield

*One of the world's largest cathedral domes*

A staircase in the southern transept leads to the Crypt, Treasury and OBE Chapel. The **Crypt** has memorials to up to 300 military demigods, including Wellington, Kitchener and Nelson. The memorial to Wren is in the **OBE Chapel**. The **Treasury** displays some of the cathedral's plate, along with some spectacularly worked vestments.

### To the People

Just outside the northern transept in St Paul's Churchyard stands a monument unveiled in 1999 to the people of London – not all those warmongers, sabre-rattlers and heroes at rest in the Crypt. Simple but elegant, it honours the 32,000 civilians killed (and another 50,000 seriously injured) in the defence of the city during WWII. The inscription asks passers-by to 'Remember before God, the people of London 1939-1945'.

## SCIENCE MUSEUM (2, G5)

The Science Museum is at the cutting edge of exhibiting items on a subject that could otherwise be quite dull. On the ground floor, **Making the Modern World** looks back at the history of the Industrial Revolution via examples of its machinery and then looks forward to the exploration of space. There are enough old trains (including **Puffing Billy**, a steam locomotive from 1813) and vintage cars to keep the kids well and truly happy.

Up a floor and you can find out about the impact of science on food, time, telecommunications and weather. Up another one and you're into the world of computers, chemistry and nuclear power. The 3rd floor is the place to come for old aeroplanes, among them the **Vickers Vimy** in which Alcock and Brown first flew the Atlantic in 1919, and Amy Johnson's *Gipsy Moth* in which she flew to Australia in 1930. On the 4th and 5th floors you'll find exhibits relating to the history of medicine and veterinary science.

The basement has imaginative **hands-on galleries for children**: the Garden is for three- to six-year-olds, Things is for seven- to 11-year-olds. The Secret Life of the Home, a collection of labour-saving appliances that householders have either embraced or shunned, is for everyone.

The new **Wellcome Wing** is filled with hands-on displays and a great place to take kids. Especially interesting is Digitopolis, which focuses on digital technology. The **IMAX cinema** has the usual crop of 3-D travelogues, space adventures and dinosaur attacks.

Simon Bracken

**INFORMATION**

✉ Exhibition Rd SW7
☎ 0870 870 4868
[e] www.sciencemuseum.org.uk
⊖ South Kensington
🕘 10am-6pm (museum & IMAX cinema)
[$] museum free; IMAX cinema £6.75/5.75 a/s&st&c
♿ excellent
🍴 Deep Blue Café

Simon Bracken

*The Science Museum's site since 1899*

**DON'T MISS**

• Apollo 10 Command Module • Boulton & Watt's steam engine • Flight Lab simulator • Foucault's Pendulum • Wells Cathedral clock (1392)

## SHAKESPEARE'S GLOBE (3, G11)

Shakespeare's Globe consists of the reconstructed Globe Theatre and an **exhibition on Elizabethan London** (the exhibits devoted to Elizabethan special effects are especially interesting) and the struggle to get the theatre rebuilt. The original Globe, dubbed the 'Wooden O' for its circular shape and roofless centre, was erected in 1599, burned down in 1613 and immediately rebuilt. In 1642 it was finally closed by the Puritans, who regarded theatres as dreadful dens of iniquity, and it was later dismantled.

Today's Globe was painstakingly restored with 600 oak pegs (there's not a nail or a screw in the house), specially fired Tudor bricks and Norfolk thatching reeds (which, for some reason, pigeons don't like); even the plaster contains goat hair, lime and sand as it did in the 17th century. Unlike other venues for Shakespearean plays, this theatre has been designed to resemble the original as closely as possible – even if that means leaving the arena open to the skies and obstructing much of the view from the seats closest to the stage with two enormous (and original) Corinthian pillars.

Although there are wooden bench seats in tiers around the stage, many people emulate the 17th-century 'groundlings' who stood in front of the stage, shouting, cajoling and moving around as the mood took them. Plays are staged at the Globe only in the warmer months; there will soon be performances in winter at the new indoor **Inigo Jones Theatre**, a replica of a Jacobean playhouse connected to the Globe.

### INFORMATION

✉ 21 New Globe Walk SE1
☎ 7902 1500
[e] www.shakespeares-globe.org
⊖ London Bridge
🕘 May-Sept: 9am-5pm; Oct-Apr 10am-5pm (exhibition & theatre tour); May-Sept: 7.30pm (performances)
$ £7.50/6/5/23 a/s&st/c/f; theatre seats £9-27, standing room £5
♿ good
🍴 The Globe Cafe, Globe Restaurant

Simon Bracken

### Wanamaker's Dream

The Globe was just a historical footnote when American actor (later film director) Sam Wanamaker came searching for it in 1949. Though the theatre's original foundations had vanished beneath a row of listed Georgian houses, Wanamaker set up the Globe Playhouse Trust in 1970 and began fund-raising for a memorial theatre. Work started in 1987, but Wanamaker died four years before it opened in 1997.

Charlotte Hindle

## TATE BRITAIN (2, H9)

The Tate Britain serves as the historical archive of British art from the early 16th century to the present day. Its sister gallery, the **Tate Modern** (p. 30), is at Bankside. Built on the site of the Millbank Penitentiary by Sidney RJ Smith in 1897 and funded by sugar magnate Sir Henry Tate, the gallery has expanded in recent years as the Tate Britain and the new **Linbury Galleries**, for the most part reserved for temporary exhibits, have increased space by more than a third. With all the moving about it is impossible to say what will be on display (and where) but likely highlights include the **Constable Gallery**, the **Gainsborough Octagon**, the Reynolds, Spencers and Hockneys in the **Painters in Focus Gallery** and the **Portrait Gallery**, with works by Whistler, Bacon and Spencer. The Tate Britain also has important works by Blake, Hogarth, Rossetti and all those stuffy paintings of thoroughbred racehorses by the pre-Victorian artist George Stubbs.

Adjoining the main building is the **Clore Gallery**, James Stirling's stab at acceptable, postmodern architecture, where the bulk of JMW Turner's paintings can be found.

Neil Setchfield

**INFORMATION**

- ✉ Millbank SW1
- ☎ 7887 8008, 7887 8888
- [e] www.tate.org.uk
- ⊖ Pimlico
- 🕘 10am-5.50pm
- $ free
- ♿ excellent
- 🍴 Tate Café & Espresso Bar, Tate Restaurant

Neil Setchfield

*Tate Britain: the national gallery of British art*

**DON'T MISS**

• Constable's *The Haywain* • Hogarth's *The Roast Beef of Old England* • Rossetti's *Girlhood of Mary the Virgin* • Stubbs' *Mares & Foals* • Turner's *The Shipwreck*

## TATE MODERN (3, G11)

Housed in the **Bankside Power Station**, designed by Giles Gilbert Scott after WWII but decommissioned in 1986, the vastly popular Tate Modern contains Britain's collection of international 20th-century and modern art.

The museum was the surprising winner of the millennium projects' popularity contest: by the end of its first year it had attracted 5.2 million visitors, making it the second favourite attraction in London after the august and long-established British Museum. As a result, opening hours have been extended and the crowds just keep on coming.

On display are high-quality works by Picasso, Matisse, Cézanne, Pollock, Rothko, Warhol and many more arranged by theme rather than chronologically or by artist.

The Tate's reputation for avant-garde special exhibitions – firmly established at its Millbank site (now the **Tate Britain**; p. 29) – continues south of the river, with recent exhibits focusing on the Italian Arte Povera (Poor Art) school of the late 60s and the sculptures of the late Juan Muñoz.

The building itself – with its two upper floors shrouded in glass and brightly lit at night and its landmark central chimney – is quite dramatic, especially when viewed from the opposite bank or the Millennium Bridge. Designed by Herzog & De Meuron (1999) it won the Pritzker award, architecture's Nobel Prize, in 2000.

**INFORMATION**

- ✉ Queen's Walk SE1
- ☎ 7887 8000
- [e] www.tate.org.uk
- ⊖ Blackfriars, London Bridge
- 🕘 Sun-Thurs 10am-6pm, Fri & Sat 10am-10pm
- $ free
- ⓘ audioguide (£1); free 1hr tours 10.30am, 11.30am, 2.30pm, 3.30pm
- ♿ excellent
- 🍴 Tate Modern Café: L2

Neil Setchfield

Neil Setchfield

*Turbine Hall: Tate Modern's breathtaking entrance*

**DON'T MISS**

• Léger's *The Mechanical Ballet* • Sam Taylor-Wood's *Brontosaurus* • Louise Bourgeois' *Insomnia* • Henry Moore's *Atom Piece* • Monet's *Water Lilies* • Richard Long's *Red Slate Circle* • Turbine Hall

# TOWER OF LONDON                    (3, F15)

One of London's three World Heritage Sites (the others are Westminster Abbey and its surrounding buildings, and Maritime Greenwich), the Tower of London has dominated the south-eastern corner of the City of London since 1078 when William the Conqueror laid the first stone of the **White Tower**. Over the next couple of centuries, more towers, a moat, a riverside wharf and a palace were added.

After Henry VIII relocated to Whitehall Palace in 1529, the tower's role as a prison became increasingly important. Sir Thomas More, two of Henry VIII's wives (Anne Boleyn and Catherine Howard), Lady Jane Grey and Princess (later Queen) Elizabeth, were just some of the more celebrated Tudor prisoners. You can see the

## INFORMATION

- ✉ Tower Hill EC3
- ☎ 7709 0765
- e www.hrp.org.uk
- ⊖ Tower Hill
- ⏰ Mar-Oct: Mon-Sat 9am-5pm, Sun 10am-5pm; Nov-Feb: Tues-Sat 9am-4pm, Sun & Mon 10am-4pm
- $ £11.30/8.50/7.50/34 a/s&st/c/f
- ⓘ audioguide (£3); free 1hr Beefeater tours every 30mins 9.30am-3.30pm (Sun from 10am, Nov-Feb to 2.30pm)
- ♿ fair
- ✕ Cafe Spice Namaste (p. 73)

Neil Setchfield

## Ravens & Beefeaters

Legend has it that should the ravens fly away, the White Tower will crumble and a great disaster will befall England. So the Tudor-costumed Yeoman Warders (Beefeaters) guarding the Tower take the safe option and clip the birds' wings. But why Beefeaters? In the 17th century the guards received a daily ration of beer and beef, a luxury beyond the reach of the poor. And so the envious nickname was born.

Neil Setchfield

**Queen's House** where Anne Boleyn is believed to have been imprisoned, and nearby the infamous **Bloody Tower** where Edward V and his younger brother were allegedly murdered by their uncle, Richard III.

A neo-Gothic barracks, now housing the **Crown Jewels**, replaced the Grand Storehouse when it burned down in 1841. Since Prince Albert oversaw the repair of the medieval towers and demolition of some of the newer buildings, the Tower of London's gruesome history became little more than the tourist attraction it is today. However, prisoners were occasionally kept here up to WWII, most notably Rudolf Hess in 1941.

# VICTORIA & ALBERT MUSEUM (2, H5)

This vast, rambling, wonderful museum of decorative art and design was created after the Great Exhibition of 1851. Amazingly, most of the V&A's collection of four million items is actually on display, so as soon as you're through the turnstile look at the floor plan and decide what you're most interested in – and stick to it.

**Level A** is mostly devoted to art and design from Asia, as well as European art. Room 40 is devoted to costume – everything from absurd 18th-century wigs and whalebone corsets to the platform shoes that brought Naomi Campbell crashing to the Paris catwalk.

**INFORMATION**

✉ Cromwell Rd SW7
☎ 7942 2000
[e] www.vam.ac.uk
⊖ South Kensington
🕘 Mon-Tues & Thurs-Sun 10am-5.45pm, Wed & last Fri of month 10am-10pm
$ free
ⓘ free 1hr tours 10.30am-3.30pm (plus Wed 4.30pm)
♿ excellent
🍴 The New Restaurant at the V&A

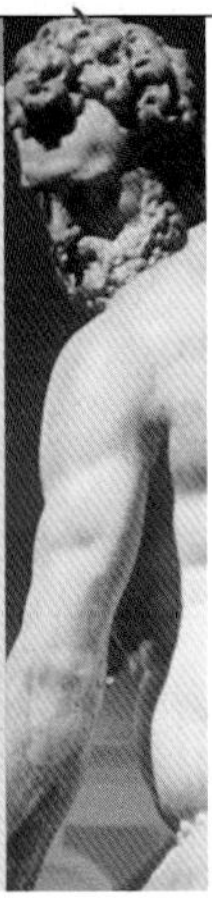
Simon Bracken

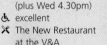

Room 48A has Raphael's sketches that formed the designs for tapestries now hanging in the Vatican Museum. Also on this level are three 1860s refreshment rooms, including the gorgeous **Green Dining Room** designed by William Morris and his friend Edward Burne-Jones.

On **Level B** are collections of ironwork (rooms 113 and 114), stained glass (rooms 11 and 116) jewellery (rooms 91 to 93) and an impressive exhibition of musical instruments (40A). In the newly renovated **British Galleries**, featuring every aspect of British design from 1500 to 1900, you will see the late-16th-century **Great Bed of Ware**, big enough to sleep five and designed as an early advertising gimmick for a Hertfordshire inn. The highlights of this floor, though, are the **Silver Galleries** (rooms 65 to 69). Up on Levels C and D are more displays of British art and design, along with ceramics, glass and porcelain from Europe and Asia. The **Henry Cole Wing** contains the largest collection of Constables gathered under one roof.

Neil Setchfield

*The V&A Museum, established in 1852*

**DON'T MISS**

• Becket Casket • *Boar and Bear Hunt* tapestry • George Gilbert Scott's Hereford Screen • Norfolk House Music Room • Maharaja Ranjit Singh's throne

# WESTMINSTER ABBEY                    (3, J6)

So rich in history is the abbey that you'll need half a day to do it justice. It's celebrated as the resting place of monarchs and the venue for great pageants. The **Coronation Chair**, where all monarchs except Edward V and Edward VIII have supposedly been crowned since 1066, is behind the main altar. Also within its walls is the nation's largest collection of tombs of politicians, poets, scientists and musicians.

The abbey, though a spectacular mix of architectural styles, is the best example of Early English Gothic in existence. The original church was built by Edward the Confessor, later St Edward, who is buried in the chapel behind the main altar. Henry III began work on the new building in the 13th century but didn't complete it; the French Gothic nave was not completed until 1388. **Henry VII's Chapel** was added in

INFORMATION

⊠ Dean's Yard SW1
☎ 7222 5152
ⓔ www.westminster-abbey.org
⊖ Westminster
⊘ Mon-Fri 9am-4.45pm, Sat 9am-2.45pm, evensong Mon-Fri 5pm & Sat-Sun 3pm
⑩ £6/3/12 a/s&st&c/f
ⓘ audioguide (£2); 1½hr tours (£3) Mon-Sat 3-6/day
⅋ good
✕ Westminster Arms

1519. Above the exit (west door) are two towers built by Sir Christopher Wren and his pupil Nicholas Hawksmoor. Just above this door stand 10 stone statues of **20th-century martyrs**, which were unveiled in 1998 and count Martin Luther King Jr and St Maxmilian Kolbe among them. Separate museums around the **Cloister** are the **Chapter House**, the **Abbey Museum** and the **Pyx Chamber**, once the Royal Treasury. These are open similar hours to the abbey.

One of the best ways to visit the abbey is to attend a service; the atmosphere and acoustics at **evensong** are awesome and inspiring.

*Westminster Abbey, the setting for every coronation since 1066*

**DON'T MISS**

●College Garden ● Poet's Corner ● Queen Elizabeth Chapel ● Quire (chancel) ● Tomb of Mary Queen of Scots

# sights & activities

## NEIGHBOURHOODS

Whoever said that London was a 'collection of villages' drew the city map for all eternity; the British capital is and forever will be a daunting patchwork of neighbourhoods, districts and quarters that retain their unique characteristics, peculiarities and, of course, loyalties. It's not uncommon for resident Londoners to refuse to 'travel' except for work, preferring to socialise, shop and entertain themselves in their own 'villages'.

### Central London

With boroughs and districts as diverse as Soho, Mayfair, Pimlico and the City, central London is a difficult area to encapsulate. **Soho** and adjoining **Covent Garden** are the epicentres of dining and nightlife in the capital, but much of it is now spilling over Oxford St into **Fitzrovia**, in an area dubbed 'Noho' and full of trendy bars and media lovelies. To the north and north-east are **Bloomsbury**, a land of B&Bs and university students, and **Holborn**, the centre of the legal profession.

The **City of London**, the 'Square Mile' of brokers and bankers, lies to the east; once you head south-west from Soho, you enter big-ticket areas such as **Mayfair**, **Piccadilly** and **St James's**, home to some of the capital's most luxurious hotels and regal residents. South of here are **Westminster**, the seat of government, and residential **Pimlico**. To the north are **Marylebone** and **Edgware Road**, nicknamed 'Little Beirut' for the preponderance of Lebanese and other Middle Eastern restaurants and cafes.

### Off the Beaten Track

It is possible to avoid the crowds in this populous city. The following are sights and attractions that most Londoners haven't even visited:

- Chelsea Physic Garden (p. 42)
- City Farms (p. 45)
- Dennis Severs' House (p. 46)
- Dulwich Picture Gallery (p. 38)
- Eltham Palace (p. 40)
- Geffrye Museum (p. 36)
- Sutton House (p. 37)
- Victoria Park (p. 43)
- Wallace Collection (p. 38)

*Sutton House: the East End's oldest house*

Neil Setchfield

### North London

The northern boroughs form an equally disparate quilt, with neighbourhoods as different as Stoke Newington, Islington, Camden and Highgate.

Central **Islington** has the lion's share of restaurants, bars and clubs especially popular with suburban young bloods, though **Stoke Newington**, less convenient and more 'alternative', is catching up. Multi-ethnic **Camden**, with its celebrated market the big draw, sits side by side with **Primrose Hill**, the closest London gets to Paris. **Hampstead**, the well-to-do 'village' nestling to the south-west of the heath, and the even more affluent **Highgate** to the north, are north London's 'blue chip' districts.

## South London

For centuries the Thames has been both south London's lifeline and its noose, creating both a real and an imaginary barrier between north and south. In recent years, the revitalised **South Bank**, with its Tate Modern, Globe Theatre and Millennium Wheel, has helped bridge the psychological gap.

**Brixton**, a focus of Caribbean immigration after WWII, is as colourful and exotic a district as you'll find, while nearby **Stockwell** is home to the city's Portuguese community. Bourgeois **Battersea**, a leafy borough by a large park to the west, feels almost country-like at times; farther south is **Clapham**, with its enormous common and one of the busiest railway crossings in the city.

## East London

The east London districts of Shoreditch, Hoxton, Spitalfields and Whitechapel may lie within walking distance of the City, but the change of pace and style is extraordinary. Traditionally this was working-class London, an area settled by waves of immigrants, though its face, too, is rapidly being rearranged.

The first areas to gentrify were **Clerkenwell** and **Farringdon**, historic but under-utilised areas just north of the City. Farther east, what were the less-than-salubrious districts of **Hoxton** and **Shoreditch** have become entertainment meccas and their loft-filled conversions very desirable addresses. Nearby **Brick Lane**, in what has become known as Bangla Town, is lined with Indian and Bangladeshi curry houses, ethnic greengrocers and leather-goods shops. Even poor **Hackney**, with its renovated Edwardian music hall, the Hackney Empire and new Ocean entertainment complex is being called 'the new Islington'. Two new towers in the **Docklands** alongside Canary Wharf are helping to attract more than just commuting bankers and journalists.

## West London

In the early 18th century, the influx of foreign immigrants to east and south London saw more affluent Londoners fleeing north and, to a greater extent, west. Places such as **Chelsea**, **South Kensington** and **Knightsbridge** became synonymous with 'posh' – as they remain today.

Neighbourhoods farther afield such as **Fulham** are less homogenous and have a mix of residents from taxi drivers to upper management. **Hammersmith** is not an especially inviting borough, though there are worse ways of spending a sunny Sunday afternoon than at one of the riverside pubs along the Upper Mall. Bordering it to the north, **Shepherd's Bush** is more workaday. **Notting Hill**, traditionally home to a multicultural mix (mostly Afro-Caribbean), has been undergoing a transformation of almost the same magnitude as east London's, ever since *that* film put it on the world map and drove up property prices.

# MUSEUMS

London boasts many smaller, more accessible museums catering to every taste and individual – from train spotters, thespians and gardeners to Surrealists and caffeine-freaks. They're spread out across town but well worth an easy tube or bus ride.

**Bethnal Green Museum of Childhood** (2, D14)
See p. 44.

**Bramah Museum of Tea & Coffee** (3, H15)
An insight into the history of tea- and coffee-drinking in the UK; nearby Butler's Wharf once handled 6000 chests of tea a day.
**✉ 1 Maguire St SE1 ☎ 7403 5650 ⊖ Tower Hill 🕒 10am-6pm $ £4/3/10 a/s&st/f ♿ good**

Simon Bracken
*It's for you, Winston.*

**Cabinet War Rooms**
(3, H6) The British government took refuge here during WWII, conducting its business from beneath 3m of solid concrete. It was from here that Winston Churchill made some of his most stirring speeches.
**✉ Clive Steps, King Charles St SW1 ☎ 7930 6961 [e] www.iwm.org.uk ⊖ Westminster 🕒 May-Sept 9.30am-6pm, Oct-Apr 10am-6pm $ free ♿ excellent**

**Dalí Universe** (3, H8)
With more than 500 items on display – from melting clocks to the famous Mae West Lips Sofa – there's something here for the Surrealist within all of us.
**✉ County Hall, Westminster Bridge Rd SE1 ☎ 7620 2720 [e] www.daliuniverse.com ⊖ Waterloo, Westminster 🕒 10am-6.30pm $ £8.50/6.50/5/22 a/s&st/c/f ♿ excellent**

**Design Museum**
(3, H15) Sir Terence Conran's sparkling white Design Museum shows how product design has evolved and how it can make the difference between success and failure for items intended for mass production.
**✉ 28 Shad Thames SE1 ☎ 7940 8790 [e] www.designmuseum.org ⊖ Tower Hill 🕒 10am-5.45pm $ £6/4/16 a/st&c/f ♿ good**

**Geffrye Museum**
(3, A15) What were once 14 almshouses are now devoted to domestic interiors, with each room furnished to show how wealthier homes would have looked from Elizabethan times right through to today.
**✉ 136 Kingsland Rd E2 ☎ 7739 9893 [e] www.geffrye-museum.org.uk ⊖ Old Street, then bus 243 🚆 Dalston Kingsland 🕒 Tues-Sat 10am-5pm, Sun 12-5pm $ free ♿ excellent**

**Horniman Museum**
**(1, C5)** This extraordinary little museum includes the Music Room with instruments and their recordings; the Living Waters Aquarium; and African Worlds, the UK's first permanent gallery of African and Afro-Caribbean art and culture.
**✉ 100 London Rd SE23 ☎ 8699 1872 🚆 Forest Hill 🕒 Mon-Sat 10.30am-5.30pm, Sun 2-5.30pm $ free ♿ excellent**

**Jewish Museum**
(4, K4) Judaism and Judaic practices are examined in the Ceremonial Art Gallery and the UK Jewish community's story from the time of the Normans is told in the History Gallery.
**✉ 129-131 Albert St NW1 ☎ 7284 1997 [e] www.jewmusm.ort.org ⊖ Camden Town 🕒 Mon-Thurs 10am-4pm, Sun 10am-5pm $ £3.50/2.50/1.50/8 a/s/st&c/f ♿ excellent**

**Kenwood House**
(4, C4) Housed in a neo-classical mansion, this museum contains what is arguably London's finest small collection of European art.
**✉ Hampstead La NW3 ☎ 8348 1286 [e] www.english-heritage.org.uk ⊖ Archway or Golders Green, then bus 210 🕒 house: Apr-Sept 10am-6pm, Oct 10am-5pm, Nov-Mar 10am-4pm; grounds: Apr-Sept**

8am-8.30pm, Oct-Mar 8am-4.35pm $ free ♿ good

**London's Transport Museum** (6, C8)
This museum explains how London made the transition from streets choked with horse-drawn carriages to the Docklands Light Rail (DLR) and the ultramodern Jubilee Line extension – a more interesting story than you might suspect.
✉ **Covent Garden Piazza WC2 ☎ 7565 7299 [e] www.lt museum.co.uk ⊖ Covent Garden 🕘 Sat-Thurs 10am-6pm, Fri 11am-6pm $ £5.95/3.95/free a/s&st/c ♿ good**

**Museum in Docklands** (p. 49)
This long-awaited museum with the slightly odd name focuses on the history of the Thames, its port and its industries.
✉ **Warehouse No 1, West India Quay E14 ☎ 7001 9800 [e] www .museumindocklands .org.uk ⊖ Canary Wharf 🚆 DLR West India Quay 🕘 10am-6pm $ £5 ♿ good**

**Museum of Gardening History** (3, K8)
This lovely place housed in a disused church was inspired by the work of the Tradescants, a father and son team who roamed the globe in search of exotic plants. There is a 17th-century replica knot garden in the small churchyard.
✉ **Lambeth Palace Rd SE1 ☎ 7401 8865 [e] www.museumgarden history.org ⊖ Lambeth North 🕘 Feb–mid-Dec 10.30am-5pm $ free ♿ good**

**Museum of London**
(3, D11) This fascinating place – the world's largest urban history museum, with more than one million objects on display and in its archives – describes how the city has evolved from the Ice Age to the Internet. Worth a visit before you tour.
✉ **London Wall EC2 ☎ 7600 3699, 7600 0807 [e] www.museum oflondon.org.uk ⊖ Barbican 🕘 Mon-Sat 10am-5.50pm, Sun 12-5.50pm $ free ♿ excellent**

**St John's Gate** (3, C10)
What looks like a toy-town medieval gate is actually the real thing, dating from the early 16th century but heavily restored 300 years later. Inside there's a museum about the Order of St John, knights who took on a nursing role during the Crusades.
✉ **St John's La EC1 ☎ 7253 6644 ⊖ Farringdon 🕘 Mon-Fri 10am-5pm, Sat 10am-4pm; tours Tues, Fri & Sat 11am & 2.30pm $ free; tours £4/3 a/s&st ♿ fair**

**Sherlock Holmes Museum** (3, C1)
Fans of Sir Arthur Conan Doyle's books will enjoy three floors of reconstructed Victoriana and the new waxworks of various Holmes characters, though our hero Holmes actually 'lived' in the Abbey National building farther south on the corner with Melcombe St.
✉ **221b Baker St NW1 ☎ 7935 8866 [e] www .sherlock-holmes.co.uk ⊖ Baker Street 🕘 9.30am-6pm $ £6/4 a/c**

**Sir John Soane's Museum** (6, A9)
See p. 46.

**Sutton House** (2, A14)
A red-brick Tudor structure originally built in 1535, this is London's oldest house and has Tudor, Stuart and Georgian interiors and gardens.
✉ **2 & 4 Homerton High St E9 ☎ 8986 2264 [e] www.national trust.org.uk 🚆 Hackney Central 🕘 Feb-Nov: Wed & Sun 11.30am-5.30pm $ £2.10/60p/ 4.80 a/c/f ♿ fair**

**Theatre Museum**
(6, C8) A branch of the Victoria & Albert Museum, this colourful museum displays costumes and artefacts relating to the history of the theatre, opera and ballet. There's a fascinating collection of memorabilia belonging to great thespians of the past.
✉ **7 Russell St WC2 ☎ 7943 4700 [e] www .theatremuseum.org ⊖ Covent Garden 🕘 Tues-Sun 10am-6pm $ free ♿ excellent**

**Wimbledon Lawn Tennis Museum** (1, C4)
On display is the history of tennis, from the crucial invention of the lawnmower (in 1830) and of the India rubber ball (in the 1850s). A state-of-the-art presentation lets fans relive their favourite moments.
✉ **Gate 4, Church Rd SW19 ☎ 8946 6131 [e] www.wimbledon.org ⊖ Southfields, Wimbledon Park 🕘 10.30am-5pm $ £5/4.25/3.50 a/s&st/c ♿ excellent**

# GALLERIES

Important fine-art groupings can be found not just in museums but in London's galleries, collections and academies as well. But what's in a name? There are also scores of smaller, often commercial galleries that host exhibitions throughout the year.

**Bankside Gallery**
**(3, G11)** Home to the Royal Watercolour Society and the Royal Society of Painter-Printmakers, this friendly, upbeat place has no permanent collection but hosts frequently changing exhibitions of watercolours, prints and engravings.
**✉ 48 Hopton St SE1 ☎ 7928 7521 [e] www.banksidegallery.com ⊖ Blackfriars, Waterloo 🕘 Tues 10am-8pm, Wed-Fri 10am-5pm, Sat-Sun 11am-5pm $ £3.50/2 a/s&st ♿ excellent**

**What's On Where?**
For information on the ever-changing exhibitions at London's commercial galleries, pick up a copy of the freebie *New Exhibitions of Contemporary Art* ([e] www.newexhibitions.com), published weekly and available in most art spaces.

**Dulwich Picture Gallery** (2, C3)
The UK's oldest public art gallery (1811) was designed by Soane for paintings collected by dealer Noel Desenfans and painter Francis Bourgeois, who are buried here. See masterpieces by Rembrandt, Rubens, Reynolds, Gainsborough and Lely.
**✉ Gallery Rd SE21 ☎ 8693 5254 [e] www.dulwichpicturegallery.org.uk 🚆 West Dulwich 🕘 Tues-Fri 10am-5pm, Sat-Sun 11am-5pm $ £4/3 a/s&st; Fri free ♿ good**

**Hayward Gallery**
**(6, E9)** Arguably London's greatest eyesore from the outside, the Hayward is also its premier exhibition space for major international art shows and has excellent hanging spaces for contemporary and 20th-century art.
**✉ Belvedere Rd SW1 ☎ 7261 0127, 7960 4242 [e] www.sbc.org.uk ⊖ Waterloo 🕘 Mon & Thurs-Sun 10am-6pm, Tues-Wed 10am-8pm $ prices vary ♿ good**

**National Portrait Gallery** (6, D6)
Put faces to both the famous and infamous names in British history. You'll find oil paintings, watercolours, drawings, sculptures, silhouettes, photographs and even electronic art.
**✉ 2 St Martin's Pl WC2 ☎ 7312 2463 [e] www.npg.org.uk ⊖ Charing Cross, Leicester Square 🕘 Mon-Wed & Sat-Sun 10am-6pm, Thurs-Fri 10am-9pm $ free ♿ good**

**Royal Academy of Arts** (6, D3)
The academy has hosted some record-breaking exhibitions in recent years. The Summer Exhibition, a show open to all entrants and held from early June to mid-August, is hugely popular.
**✉ Burlington House, Piccadilly W1 ☎ 7300 8000 [e] www.royalacademy.org.uk ⊖ Green Park 🕘 Mon-Thurs & Sat-Sun 10am-6pm, Fri 10am-8.30pm $ prices vary ♿ excellent**

**Saatchi Gallery** (2, C4)
Not the place to come if your tastes run to Constable or Turner; you're likely to find giant pools of oil reflecting the ceiling or scarily lifelike models of human figures. The space is light, airy and large.
**✉ 98a Boundary Rd NW8 ☎ 7624 8299 ⊖ Kilburn High Road 🕘 Thurs-Sun 12-6pm $ £5/3 a/s&st&c ♿ good**

**Wallace Collection**
**(3, D2)** London's finest small gallery is a treasure-trove of paintings from the 17th and 18th centuries in a splendid Italianate mansion. There are works by Rubens, Titian, Poussin, Frans Hals and Rembrandt; four new galleries in the basement focus on watercolours and conservation.
**✉ Hertford House, Manchester Sq W1 ☎ 7935 9500 [e] www.wallace-collection.com ⊖ Bond Street 🕘 Mon-Sat 10am-5pm, Sun 12-5pm $ free ♿ excellent**

# NOTABLE BUILDINGS & MONUMENTS

**Albert Memorial** (2, G5) This over-the-top monument to Queen Victoria's German husband Albert (1819-61) was taken out of wraps in 1998 after an £11-million renovation lasting eight years.
**✉ Hyde Park, Kensington Gore SW7 ☎ 7495 0916 ⊖ South Kensington, Gloucester Road 🕐 tours Sun 2pm & 3pm $ £3.50/3 a/s&st ♿ good**

**British Library** (3, A6) The British Library, which moved to its new home in 1998, stocks every British publication in print as well as historical manuscripts, books and maps. It has the Magna Carta, a Gutenberg Bible, Shakespeare's First Folio and many other priceless documents on exhibit.
**✉ 96 Euston Rd NW1 ☎ 7412 7000, 7412 7332 [e] www.bl.uk ⊖ King's Cross 🕐 Mon & Wed-Fri 9.30am-6pm, Tues 9.30am-8pm, Sat 9.30am-5pm, Sun 11am-5pm $ free ♿ excellent**

**The Monument** (3, F13) This 60m stone column topped with a gilded bronze urn of flames was designed by Wren to commemorate the Great Fire, which started in a bakery nearby in 1666. Tight steps (all 311 of them) lead to a balcony beneath the urn offering panoramic views over the City.
**✉ Monument St EC3 ☎ 7626 2717 ⊖ Monument 🕐 10am-5.40pm $ £1.50/50p a/c**

**Old Royal Naval College** (5, C3) This Wren masterpiece is now used by the University of Greenwich. However, you can still view the fabulous Painted Hall in the King William Building and the Chapel in the Queen Mary Building.
**✉ King William Walk SE10 ☎ 0800 389 3341, 8269 4747 🚆 DLR Cutty Sark 🕐 Mon-Sat 10am-5pm, Sun 12.30pm-5pm $ £3/2 (free after 3.30pm & all day Sun) ♿ fair**

**Prince Henry's Room** (6, B10) The building containing this small museum dates from the 16th century but was remodelled as a tavern with an overhanging half-timbered facade in 1611. The 1st-floor room, with items related to the life and writings of Samuel Pepys, boasts the best Jacobean plaster ceiling extant in London.
**✉ 17 Fleet St EC4 ☎ 7936 2710 ⊖ Temple 🕐 Mon-Sat 11am-2pm $ free**

**Royal Observatory** (5, D3) Since 1884, Greenwich Mean Time (GMT) has been accepted as the universal measurement of standard time. It's here that the globe divides between east and west, and you can place one foot either side of the meridian line and straddle the two hemispheres.
**✉ Greenwich Park SE10 ☎ 8312 6565 [e] www.nmm.ac.uk 🚆 DLR Cutty Sark 🕐 Apr-Sept 10am-6pm, Oct-Mar 10am-5pm $ free ♿ good**

**Tower Bridge** (3, G15) Visitors reach the top of one of this Victorian folly's 25m-high twin towers by lift, and the walkways afford excellent views across the City and Docklands.
**✉ Tower Bridge SE1 ☎ 7940 3985 [e] www.towerbridge.org.uk ⊖ Tower Hill 🕐 Apr-Oct 10am-6.30pm, Nov-Mar 9.30am-6pm $ £6.25/4.25/18.25-22.25 a/s&st&c/f ♿ good**

**Wellington Arch** (3, H2) Built in 1826 to commemorate Wellington's victories over Napoleon, the arch has three floors of exhibition space and a viewing platform with spectacular vistas of the park and Houses of Parliament.
**✉ Hyde Park Cnr W1 ☎ 7973 3292 [e] www.english-heritage.org.uk ⊖ Hyde Park Corner 🕐 Wed-Sun 10am-6pm $ £2.50/1.90/1.30 a/s&st/c ♿ good**

Neil Setchfield

*The towering Tower Bridge*

# FAMOUS ABODES

**Carlyle's House** (2, J5)
The great essayist and historian Thomas Carlyle wrote his famous history of the French Revolution and many other works in this Queen Anne residence.
**✉ 24 Cheyne Row SW3 ☎ 7352 7087 ⊖ Sloane Square ⏰ Apr-early Nov: Wed-Sun 11am-5pm $ £3.50/1.75 a/c**

**Dickens' House** (3, C8)
This is London's only surviving residence of the many lived in by the great Victorian novelist. He wrote *The Pickwick Papers*, *Nicholas Nickleby* and *Oliver Twist* during his two-year (1837-39) residence here.
**✉ 49 Doughty St WC1 ☎ 7405 2127 [e] www.dickensmuseum.com ⊖ Russell Square ⏰ Mon-Sat 10am-5pm $ £4/3/2/9 a/s&st/c/f**

**Dr Johnson's House** (3, E9) This well-preserved Georgian town house is where the lexicographer Dr Johnson lived from 1748 to 1759 and is full of pictures of his friends and intimates.
**✉ 17 Gough Sq EC4 ☎ 7353 3745 [e] www.drjh.dircon.co.uk ⊖ Blackfriars ⏰ May-Sept: Mon-Sat 11am-5.30pm; Oct-Apr: Mon-Sat 11am-5pm $ £4/3/1/9 a/s&st/c/f**

**Eltham Palace** (1, B5)
This stunning place is an unusual hybrid: part Tudor, part Art Deco. Henry VIII lived here as a child, and a member of the Courtauld clan built a country home onto its remains in the 1930s.
**✉ Court Rd SE9 ☎ 8294 2548 [e] www.english-heritage.org.uk 🚆 Eltham ⏰ Apr-Sept: Wed-Fri & Sun 10am-6pm; Oct: Wed-Fri & Sun 10am-5pm; Nov-Mar: Wed-Fri & Sun 10am-4pm $ house & grounds £6/4.50/3 a/s&st/c, grounds only £3.60/2.70/1.80 ♿ good**

**Freud Museum** (2, B5)
Sigmund Freud spent the last 18 months of his life here after fleeing Nazi-occupied Vienna. The house contains the psychiatrist's original couch, his books and his Greek and Asian artefacts.
**✉ 20 Maresfield Gardens NW3 ☎ 7435 2002 [e] www.freud.org.uk ⊖ Finchley Road ⏰ Wed-Sun 12-5pm $ £4/2/free a/s&st/c ♿ fair**

**Handel House Museum** (6, C1)
This new museum, the first devoted to a composer in London, celebrates the life and times of George Frideric Handel, who lived at No 25 from 1723 until his death 36 years later.
**✉ 23-25 Brook St W1 ☎ 7495 1685 ⊖ Bond Street, Oxford Circus ⏰ Tues-Wed & Fri-Sat 10am-6pm, Thurs 10am-8pm, Sun 12-6pm $ £4.50/3.50/2 a/s&st/c ♿ excellent**

**Keats' House** (2, B5)
Sitting under a plum tree in the garden inspired the Romantic poets' golden boy to write his most celebrated poem, *Ode to a Nightingale*. View original manuscripts and letters, mementoes and Keats' collection of works by Chaucer and Shakespeare.
**✉ Wentworth Pl, Keats Grove NW3 ☎ 7435 2062 [e] www.keatshouse.org.uk ⊖ Hampstead 🚆 Hampstead Heath ⏰ Nov-late Mar: Tues-Sun 12-4pm; late Mar-Oct Tues-Sun 12-5pm; tours by appointment only 10am-noon $ £3/1.50/free a/s&s/c**

**Wellington Museum** (3, H2) The striking 18th-century Apsley House overlooking Hyde Park Corner opposite Wellington Arch was home to the duke of Wellington from 1817 to 1852 and retains most of its furnishings and collections.
**✉ 149 Piccadilly W1 ☎ 7499 5676 ⊖ Hyde Park Corner ⏰ Tues-Sun 11am-5pm $ free ♿ fair**

## Blue Plaques

Placing blue plaques on the houses of distinguished Londoners began in 1867. The original criteria for the placing of a plaque were that the candidate must have been dead for at least 20 years, born more than 100 years prior and be known to the 'well-informed passer-by'.

# CHURCHES & CATHEDRALS

**Christ Church** (3, D14)
Opposite Spitalfields Market, this magnificent English Baroque church was designed by Nicholas Hawksmoor and completed in 1729 for the Huguenot weavers who lived in the area.
**✉ Commercial St E1 ☎ 7247 7202 ⊖ Shoreditch, Liverpool Street 🕐 Mon-Fri 12.30pm-2.30pm, Sun 12.30pm-4.30pm ♿ fair**

**St Bartholomew-the-Great** (3, D11)
One of London's oldest churches, St Bartholomew-the-Great has Norman arches and details that lend this holy space an ancient calm; approaching from Smithfield Market through a 13th-century archway is like walking back in time.
**✉ West Smithfield EC1 ☎ 7606 5171 [e] www.greatbarts.com ⊖ Barbican, Farringdon 🕐 Tues-Fri 8.30am-5pm, Sat 10.30am-1.30pm, Sun 8am-8pm ♿ good**

**St Bride's** (3, E10)
A small but perfect church by Wren in 1671, St Bride's is still referred to as 'the journalists' church' or 'the printers' cathedral' due to its Fleet St location. A chapel honours journalists who have been killed or injured in the course of their work.
**✉ Fleet St EC4 ☎ 7353 1301 ⊖ Blackfriars 🕐 8am-4.45pm ♿ good**

**St Martin-in-the-Fields** (6, D6)
An early 18th-century masterpiece by James Gibbs, this celebrated church occupies a prime site on Trafalgar Square and helps form one of London's greatest vistas. It has a tradition of tending to the poor and homeless that goes back to WWI.
**✉ Trafalgar Sq WC2 ☎ 7766 1199 [e] www.stmartin-in-the-fields.org ⊖ Charing Cross 🕐 8am-6.30pm ♿ good**

**St Mary-le-Bow** (3, E12)
Built in 1673, St Mary-le-Bow is famous as the church whose bells dictate who is – and who is not – a cockney; if you were born within the sound of their peal, you're the genuine article. The delicate steeple is one of Wren's finest works.
**✉ Cheapside EC2 ☎ 7248 5139 ⊖ Bank, St Paul's 🕐 Mon-Thurs 6.30am-6pm, Fri 6.30am-4pm ♿ good**

**Southwark Cathedral** (6, G13) This medieval cathedral, largely a Victorian repair job, contains a memorial to Shakespeare, the tomb of the Bard's brother, Edmond, and a new multimedia exhibition called The Long View of London, which examines London from this vantage point over the past 2000 years.
**✉ Montague Close SE1 ☎ 7367 6700 [e] www.dswark.org ⊖ London Bridge 🕐 8am-6pm; evensong Tues & Fri 5.30pm, Sat 4pm, Sun 3pm $ £2.50 donation requested ♿ good**

**Temple Church** (6, B10) Originally built by the secretive Knights Templar between 1161 and 1185, the core of the structure is the only round church left in London.
**✉ King's Bench Walk, Inner Temple EC4 ☎ 7353 8559 [e] www.templechurch.com ⊖ Temple, Blackfriars 🕐 Wed-Fri 11am-6pm, Sat 11am-2.30pm, Sun 12.45pm-2.45pm ♿ good**

**Westminster Cathedral** (3, K4)
The British headquarters of the Roman Catholic Church is the only good example of neo-Byzantine architecture in London. The views from the distinctive candy-striped red-brick and white-stone tower are phenomenal.
**✉ Victoria St SW1 ☎ 7798 9055 [e] www.westminstercathedral.org.uk ⊖ Victoria 🕐 cathedral: 7am-7pm; tower: Apr-Nov 9am-5pm, Dec-Mar Thurs-Sun 9am-5pm $ free; tower £2/1/5 a/s&c/f ♿ good**

Neil Setchfield

*Westminster Cathedral*

# PARKS & GARDENS

London boasts more parks, gardens and open spaces than any city of its size in the world.

**Battersea Park** (2, K6) Stretching out between Albert and Chelsea Bridges, this 50-hectare space of greenery is filled with attractions and distractions, most prominently the Japanese Peace Pagoda. Hire boats (£4.60) can be rowed on the lake.
**✉ Albert Bridge Rd SW11 ☎ 8871 7534 ⊖ Sloane Square, then bus 137 🕐 dawn-dusk ♿ excellent**

**Chelsea Physic Garden** (2, J6) This peaceful oasis, created by the Apothecaries' Society livery company (p. 9) in 1673 to study the relationship of botany to medicine (then known as the 'physic art'), is one of Europe's oldest botanical gardens.
**✉ 66 Royal Hospital Rd SW3 (entrance on Swan Walk) ☎ 7352 5646 [e] www.cpgarden.demon.co.uk ⊖ Sloane Square 🕐 Apr-Oct: Wed 12-5pm, Sun 2-6pm (Mon-Fri 12-5pm during Chelsea Flower Show in May) $ £4/2 a/c ♿ excellent**

**Hampstead Heath** (1, B4) The heath covers 320 hectares, most of it woods, hills and meadows. Some sections of the heath are laid out for ball sports and there are several bathing ponds.
**✉ Hampstead Heath NW3 ☎ 7485 4491 ⊖ Hampstead 🚆 Gospel Oak, Hampstead Heath 🕐 24hrs ♿ excellent**

Neil Setchfield

*Blading around London*

**Hyde Park** (2, F5) This 145-hectare park is central London's largest open space. Expropriated from the Church by Henry VIII, it became a hunting ground for kings and aristocrats, and then a venue for duels, executions, horse racing and the site of the 1851 Great Exhibition. It's a riot of colour in spring, and full of lazy sunbathers and boats on the Serpentine in summer.
**✉ Hyde Park W2 ☎ 7298 2100 ⊖ Hyde Park Corner, Knightsbridge, Lancaster Gate, Marble Arch 🕐 5.30am-midnight ♿ excellent**

**Regent's Park** (3, B2) Like most of London's other parks, this park was used as a royal hunting ground, subsequently farmed and then revived as a place for fun and leisure during the 18th century. It contains London

## London in Flower

Plant-lovers won't want to miss Kew Gardens (p. 21), but if you're more interested in less exotic plants, London's parks boast a wide range of common garden variety trees, shrubs and flowers. Many Londoners also take pride in their private gardens, some of which are open to the public for a few days each year (generally May-Sept) through the National Gardens Scheme (£1.50-2). Call ☎ 01483-211535 ([e] www.ngs.org.uk) to receive a *London Gardens* pamphlet (50p).

Neil Setchfield

*Park yourself on a bench and watch the world go by.*

Zoo (p. 42), the Grand Union Canal and an open-air theatre.
✉ **Regent's Park NW1**
☎ **7486 7905**
⊖ **Baker Street, Regent's Park** 🕘 **May-Sept: 5am-dusk**
♿ **excellent**

**Richmond Park** (1, B4)
One of London's largest (1000 hectares) and wildest parks, Richmond Park is home to all sorts of wildlife: foxes, badgers and herds of red and fallow deer. It's a great place for birdwatchers too.
✉ **Richmond, Surrey**
☎ **8948 3209**
⊖ **Richmond**
🕘 **Mar-Sept: 7am-dusk; Oct-Feb: 7.30am-dusk** ♿ **excellent**

**St James's Park**
(3, H5) The neatest and most regal of London's parks, St James's has the best vistas, including those of Westminster, Buckingham Palace and St James's Palace.
✉ **The Mall SW1**
☎ **7930 1793**
⊖ **St James's Park, Charing Cross**
🕘 **5am-dusk**
♿ **excellent**

**Victoria Park** (2, C15)
Known as 'Regent's Park in the East End', Victoria Park opened in 1850 as a playground for London's poor. It has several large ponds, a neogothic drinking fountain (1861) and statues of the mythical Dogs of Alcibiades (1912).
✉ **Sewardstone Rd E2**
☎ **8533 2057** ⊖ **Mile End, then bus 277** 🚆 **Homerton** 🕘 **7am-dusk**
♿ **excellent**

**Wetland Centre**
(2, K1) Europe's largest inland wetland project, the Wetland Centre was created from four Victorian reservoirs in 2000 and attracts some 130 species of birds and 300 types of moths and butterflies.
✉ **Queen Elizabeth's Walk SW13** ☎ **8409 4400** [e] **www.wetland centre.org.uk**
⊖ **Hammersmith, then bus 283 ('Duck Bus')** 🕘 **summer 9.30am-6pm; winter 9.30am-5pm**
$ **£6.75/5.50/4/17.50 a/s&st/c/f** ♿ **excellent**

### Speak your Mind
Every Sunday at Speakers' Corner, just south of Marble Arch in Hyde Park, anyone with a soapbox can hold forth on whatever subject takes their fancy. Unless you expect the silver-throated oratory of a modern-day Churchill, you shouldn't be disappointed.

### London's Wildlife
In addition to the Wetland Centre, London has more than 50 nature reserves maintained by the London Wildlife Trust (☎ 7261 0447, [e] www.wildlifetrust.org.uk/london). Battersea Park Nature Reserve has several nature trails, while parts of Hampstead Heath are designated Sites of Special Scientific Interest (SSSIs) for their wealth of natural history.

Neil Setchfield

*Unspoilt scenery in the depths of the city (St James's Park)*

# LONDON FOR CHILDREN

Although London's crowds, traffic and pollution might be off-putting to some parents, the city is jam-packed with things to entertain the young 'uns. The London Tourist Board's (LTB) London Line (☎ 09068 663344) can fill you in on what's on for children.

**Bethnal Green Museum of Childhood** (2, D14)
Guaranteed to entertain the kids and bring back memories of your own childhood, this museum is packed with dolls, dolls' houses, train sets, model cars, children's clothes, old board games, books, toy theatres and puppets from the 17th century to today.
✉ **Cambridge Heath Rd E2** ☎ **8980 2415** [e] **www.museumofchildhood.org.uk** ⊖ **Bethnal Green** 🕘 **Sat-Thurs 10am-5.50pm** $ **free** ♿ **good**

## Babysitting

Need a break from the ankle-biters? Contact Childminders (6, C2; ☎ 7935 2049 day, 7935 3000 night [e] www.babysitter.co.uk) at 6 Nottingham St W1.

**Chelsea World of Sport** (2, K4)
This temple to English football traces the history and achievements of Chelsea Football Club. Other interactive and virtual displays focus on tennis, volleyball, sprinting, rowing and climbing.
✉ **Chelsea Village, Fulham Rd SW6** ☎ **7915 2222** [e] **www.chelseaworldofsport.com** ⊖ **Fulham Broadway** 🕘 **Mon-Fri 10am-6pm, Sat-Sun 9am-6pm**

*Punch and Judy: the traditional children's puppet show*

$ **£12.50/8/40 a/s&c/f** ♿ **excellent**

**Cutty Sark** (5, C2)
Stroll the decks and peep inside the refitted teak-lined cabins of the beautiful *Cutty Sark* clipper, the fastest ship that had ever sailed the seven seas when launched in 1869.
✉ **Cutty Sark Gardens, King William Walk SE10** ☎ **8858 3445** 🚉 **DLR Cutty Sark** 🕘 **10am-5pm** $ **£3.50/2.50/8.50 a/c/f** ♿ **fair**

**HMS Belfast** (3, G1)
This large cruiser saw a lot of action during WWII and was decommissioned in the 1960s. Kids will love exploring the eight zones on nine decks, and scrambling up and down steep ladders.
✉ **Morgan's La, Tooley St SE1** ☎ **7940 6300** [e] **www.hmsbelfast.org.uk** ⊖ **London Bridge** 🕘 **Mar-Oct: 10am-6pm; Nov-Feb: 10am-5pm** $ **£5/3.80/12 a/s&st/f** ♿ **fair**

**London Aquarium** (3, H8) This state-of-the-art 'zoo' for fish lacks the colour and airiness of more purpose-built structures, but the coral reef display and the new terrapin tank are quite impressive.
✉ **County Hall, Westminster Bridge Rd SE1** ☎ **7967 8000** [e] **www.londonaquarium.co.uk** ⊖ **Westminster, Waterloo** 🕘 **10am-6pm** $ **£8.75/6.50/5.25/25 a/s&st/c/f** ♿ **excellent**

**London IMAX Cinema** (6, F10) This is the largest IMAX cinema in Europe, with a screen some 10 storeys high and 26m wide. The 485-seat cinema screens the usual 2-D and IMAX 3-D films – documentaries about travel, space and wildlife.
✉ **1 Charlie Chaplin Walk SE1** ☎ **7902 1234** [e] **www.bfi.org.uk/imax** ⊖ **Waterloo** 🕘 **multiple screenings 1.15pm-8pm (Fri-Sat 9.15pm)** $ **£6.95/5.95/4.95 a/s&st/c (additional films £4.20)**

**London Trocadero** (6, C4) This indoor entertainment complex, on six levels and anchored by the

Funland indoor theme park, has many high-tech rides and video games. Great for youngsters not into more cultural attractions; just don't expect a peaceful outing.

✉ **Piccadilly Circus W1**
☎ 09068 881100
e www.troc.co.uk
⊖ Piccadilly Circus
⊙ 10am-1am ⓢ £3/ride, 2/5/12/26-ride tokens £5/10/20/40
& good

### London Zoo (4, E1)
One of the world's oldest zoos, it now focuses on conservation and education and keeps far fewer species than previously, and in breeding groups if possible. Web of Life, a glass breeding pavilion containing 60 animal exhibits (from termites and jellyfish to the birds and the bees), is alone worth the visit.

✉ **Regent's Park NW1**
☎ 7722 3333 e www.londonzoo.co.uk
⊖ Camden Town
⊙ Mar-Oct: 10am-5.30pm; Nov-Feb: 10am-4pm ⓢ f10/8.50/7/30 a/s&st/c/f & good

### Thames Flood Barrier
(1, B5) Kids love the barrier. Built between Greenwich and Woolwich between 1972 and 1982 in order to protect London from

## City Farms
To demonstrate to young urban Londoners that cows' udders are not shaped like milk bottles, farms have been set up all over the city. They're more popular with local people than visitors, so they offer a good way of getting off the beaten track.

- **Coram's Fields** (3, B7) ✉ 93 Guildford St WC1 ☎ 7837 6138 ⊖ Russell Square ⊙ summer 9am-7pm, winter 9am-6pm
- **Hackney City Farm** (2, C13) ✉ 1a Goldsmith's Row E2 ☎ 7729 6381 ⊖ Bethnal Green ⊙ Tues-Sun 10am-4.30pm
- **Kentish Town City Farm** (2, A7) ✉ 1 Cressfield Close, Grafton Rd NW5 ☎ 7916 5420) ⊖ Kentish Town ⊙ Tues-Sun 9.30am-5.30pm
- **Spitalfields Farm** (2, D13) ✉ Weaver St E1 ☎ 7247 8762 ⊖ Shoreditch or Liverpool Street ⊙ Tues-Sun 10.30am-5.30pm

flooding, it consists of 11 surreal-looking movable gates supported between nine concrete piers. The mechanisms are tested once a month; ring for details.

✉ **1 Unity Way SE18**
☎ 8305 4188 e www.environment-agency.co.uk ▢ Charlton ▣ 177 or 180 from Greenwich ⚓ to/from Greenwich Pier 4 times a day Apr-Oct (3 a day Nov-Dec & Feb) ⊙ Mon-Fri 10am-5pm, Sat-Sun 10.30am-5.30pm ⓢ £3.40/2/7.50 a/s&c/f & good

### Woolwich Royal Arsenal (1, B5)
Firepower at the Woolwich Royal Arsenal recreates the experiences of artillery gunners over the past century; other exhibits include the History and Real Weapons galleries. It's loud, it flashes and the kids can't get enough of it all.

✉ **Royal Arsenal Woolwich SE18** ☎ 8855 7755 e www.firepower.org.uk ▢ Woolwich Arsenal ⊙ 10am-5pm ⓢ £ 6.50/5.50/4.50 a/s&st/c & excellent

*Teddies for tiny tourists*

Neil Setchfield

# QUIRKY LONDON

**Buddhapadipa Temple** (1, C4)
This is as authentic a Thai Buddhist temple as ever graced this side of Bangkok, complete with *wat* (temple compound) and *bot*, or consecrated chapel, decorated with traditional scenes by two leading Thai artists. Remember to take your shoes off before entering the bot.
**✉ 14 Calonne Rd SW19 ☎ 8946 1357 ⊖ Wimbledon, then bus 93 🕘 summer 8am-9.30pm, winter 8am-6pm; temple Sat 1pm-6pm, Sun 8.30am-10.30am & 12.30-6pm $ free ♿ good**

**Castle Climbing Centre** (2, A11)
It ain't Everest or even the Matterhorn but this is the UK's foremost climbing centre. For everyone from beginners to experienced climbers, it's uniquely located in an enormous neo-Gothic castle.
**✉ Green Lanes N4 ☎ 8211 7000 [e] www.castle-climbing.co.uk ⊖ Manor House 🚌 171A, 141 🕘 Mon-Fri 2pm-10pm, Sat-Sun 10am-7pm $ £6/3.50 a/c**

**Dennis Severs' House** (3, C14) This is a really odd one: a Shoreditch terraced house fully restored to its 18th-century splendour (ie, no electricity or modern plumbing) and open to visit (Mon 'Silent Night' tours are by candlelight and talking is banned).
**✉ 18 Folgate St E1 ☎ 7247 4013 [e] www.denissevershouse.co.uk ⊖ Liverpool Street 🕘 1st Sun 2pm-5pm, 1st Mon 12-2pm, every Mon eve (times vary with season) $ £5/7/10 Sun/Mon 12-2pm/Mon eve**

**Highgate Cemetery** (1, B4) This 'Victorian Valhalla' is the final resting place of Karl Marx, the novelist Mary Anne Evans (aka George Eliot), the scientist Michael Faraday, the philosopher Herbert Spencer and lots of other ordinary mortals. The more atmospheric western sector is by tour only; phone for details.
**✉ Swain's La N6 ☎ 8340 1834, ⊖ Highgate 🕘 Apr-Oct: Mon-Fri 10am-5pm, Sat-Sun 11am-5pm; Nov-Mar: Mon-Fri 10am-4pm, Sat-Sun 11am-4pm $ £2/1 a/c; tour £3/1 a/c ♿ good**

**London Dungeon** (3, G13) Watch people hanging on the Tyburn gallows, listen to Anne Boleyn pleading her case just before her head is deftly separated from her soft narrow shoulders and observe St Thomas à Becket's murder. It's still all pretty scary stuff – especially the mock-ups of the Whitechapel backstreets as Jack the Ripper knew them.
**✉ 28-34 Tooley St SE1 ☎ 09001 600066 [e] www.thedungeons.com ⊖ London Bridge 🕘 Apr-Sept 10am-6.30pm, Oct-Mar 10am-5.30pm $ £10.95/9.50/6.95 a/s&st/c ♿ good**

**Old Operating Theatre** (3, G13)
As gruesome as the London Dungeon but without the humour, this museum in a garret at the top of St Thomas' Church tower focuses on the mundane nastiness of 19th-century hospital treatment. The garret was once used by the apothecary of St Thomas' Hospital to store medicinal herbs.
**✉ 9a St Thomas St SE1 ☎ 7955 4791 [e] www.thegarret.org.uk ⊖ London Bridge 🕘 10am-5pm $ £3.50/2.50/1.75/8 a/s&st/c/f**

*A past operating table*

**Sir John Soane's Museum** (6, A9)
Partly a beautiful, if quirky, house; partly a small museum representing the personal taste of the highly regarded architect (and something of a pack-rat) John Soane (1753-1837). William Hogarth's original *Rake's Progress* is here.
**✉ 13 Lincoln's Inn Fields WC2 ☎ 7405 2107 [e] www.soane.org ⊖ Holborn 🕘 Tues-Sat 10am-5pm, plus 1st Tues of the month 6pm-9pm; tours Sat 2.30pm $ free; tours £3**

# KEEPING FIT

## Golf

Visitors can drive, chip and putt at **Chingford Golf Club** (158 Station Rd E4; 1, A5; ☎ 8529 2107 🚇 Chingford), where green fees are £10.80/£14.50 weekdays/ weekends; or at **Richmond Park Golf Course** (Roehampton Gate, Priory Lane SW15; 1, B4; ☎ 8876 3205; 🚇 Barnes) for £15/18.

**Feeling Sporty**
Sportsline (☎ 7222 8000) provides information on London's many sporting facilities.

## Gyms

If your hotel doesn't have gym facilities (and a good many don't) try **Oasis Sports Centre** (32 Endell St WC2; 6, E6; ☎ 7831 1804; ⊖ Covent Garden), a popular and central sports centre with heated indoor and outdoor 25m pools, gymnasium facilities and squash and badminton courts for casual hire. A dip will cost you £2.90 and court hire costs £5.70-8. Use of gym facilities requires a compulsory gym induction (£16 with use of fitness studio and pools; thereafter £5.40/visit).

## Horse Riding

Horses can be hired for £32/hr on weekdays and £35/hr at weekends (riding lessons: £34/hr, £300/10hrs) from **Hyde Park Stables** (63 Bathurst Mews W2; 2, F5; ☎ 7723 2813; e www.hydeparkstables.com; ⊖ Lancaster Gate).

## Pools, Spas & Baths

London once had many 'stews', or public baths, which had a distinctly dodgy reputation. Few survive today, but the ones that do are squeaky clean and worth a visit. Try the Art Deco **Porchester Spa** (Porchester Centre, Queensway W2; 2, E4; ☎ 7792 3980; ⊖ Bayswater, Royal Oak) for £18.95 (£26.75/couple). **Ironmonger Row Baths** (Ironmonger Row EC1; 3, B12; ☎ 7253 4011; ⊖ Old Street) is the closest London gets to a Turkish bath and costs £10/£6.20 afternoons & weekends/mornings. Both have separate sessions for men, women and mixed; call for details.

The city is full of places to swim; look under 'Swimming Pools' or 'Leisure Centres' in the *Yellow Pages* for public pools or try Oasis (above). Hardier souls head for the **Hampstead Heath Ponds** (☎ 7485 4491; 🚇 Hampstead Heath, Gospel Oak), open 7am-dusk year round.

## Tennis

Most London parks have courts; book in advance to secure a game. Check e www.londontennis.co.uk for where to play in your area. The **Lawn Tennis Association** (Queen's Club, Palliser Rd W14; ☎ 7381 7000; e www.lta.org.uk) produces a useful series of pamphlets on where to play tennis in London, which they'll send you on receipt of a stamped addressed envelope.

# out & about

## WALKING TOURS
### Whitehall Wander

Start at Prince Charles' residence, St James's Palace ❶. Skirt around its eastern side down Marlborough Rd and emerge in The Mall ❷, with Buckingham Palace ❸ to the west (right). Enter St James's Park ❹, cross the footbridge and follow the large lake to its eastern end. Turn south (right) into Horse Guards Rd, past the Cabinet War Rooms ❺.

Continue south and turn left into Great George St to Parliament Square and Westminster Abbey ❻. Across St Margaret St are the Houses of Parliament ❼ with the famous Clock Tower (aka Big Ben) ❽. Refuel at the *Westminster Arms* pub-restaurant ❾ (☎ 7222 8520), west across the square at 9 Storey's Gate SW1.

From Parliament Square, walk north towards Whitehall, which is lined with the grand buildings of government ministries and departments. The ordinary-looking house to the left at No 10 Downing St ❿ has accommodated UK prime ministers since 1732. Farther along to the east (right) is Banqueting House ⓫, the last remnant of the Tudor Whitehall Palace. King Charles I, accused of treason by Cromwell, was beheaded outside the house on 30 January 1649.

Finally, you arrive in Trafalgar Square ⓬, with Nelson's Column ⓭ in the centre and the National Gallery ⓮ and National Portrait Gallery ⓯ to the north. St Martin-in-the-Fields ⓰ is to the east and, to the southwest, Admiralty Arch ⓱, erected in honour of Queen Victoria in 1910.

**distance** 2.2 miles (3.5km)
**duration** 3hrs
▶ **start** ⊖ Green Park
● **end** ⊖ Charing Cross

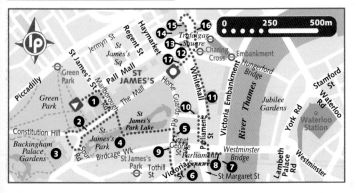

# Docklands Dawdle

Begin at the Tower of London ❶ and walk east under Tower Bridge ❷ to St Katharine's Dock ❸, the first of London's docks to be renovated (in 1968). East along the river from the dock, along St Katharine's Way, is Wapping ❹. Cobbled Wapping High St leads past Execution Dock ❺ at Wapping New Stairs, where convicted pirates (including Captain William Kidd) were hanged and their bodies chained to a post at low tide.

**SIGHTS & HIGHLIGHTS**

Tower of London (p. 31)
Tower Bridge (p. 39)
Museum in Docklands (p. 37)

*Tower Bridge detail*

Head north along Wapping Lane and across to St George-in-the-East ❻, designed by Hawksmoor in 1726. Cannon St Rd leads to Cable St, where ropes were once manufactured. Head east to the Town Hall building ❼ – now a library – which bears a mural marking the attempt by British Fascist Blackshirts to intimidate the local Jewish population in 1936.

Enter the Limehouse ❽ district by following Cable St east and north to Commercial Rd and Limehouse Rd. Current reminders of London's first Chinatown are limited to street names such as Ming and Mandarin Sts but make a noodle stop at *Old Friends* Chinese restaurant ❾ (☎ 7790 5027) at 659 Commercial Rd E14.

Head east to West India Dock Rd, leading south to the Isle of Dogs ❿, which is dominated by Cesar Pelli's 244m steel and glass colossus One Canada Square ⓫, commonly known as Canary Wharf Tower, and two new towers. The newly opened Museum in Docklands ⓬ is across the channel to the north, in one of the old warehouses next to the West India Quay DLR station.

| | |
|---|---|
| **distance** | 3.7 miles (6km) |
| **duration** | 3½hrs |
| ▶ **start** | ⊖ Tower Hill |
| ● **end** | 🚉 DLR West India Quay |

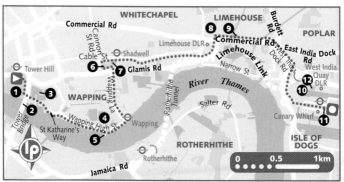

## Fleet St Footslog

Begin at busy Ludgate Circus and walk west along Fleet St; on the southern (left) side is St Bride's **1**. Farther along on the north (right) is Wine Office Court, an alleyway leading to *Ye Olde Cheshire Cheese* pub **2**.

Continue west and turn north (right) into Johnson's Court, which leads to Dr Johnson's House **3**. A bit farther along Fleet St on the southern side is *Ye Olde Cock Tavern* **4** at No 22, the oldest pub on Fleet St and a favourite of the good doctor, Pepys, Dickens and TS Eliot. Opposite stands St Dunstan-in-the-West **5**, where the figures of Gog and Magog chime bells on the hour.

Prince Henry's Room **6** is at No 17 and just beyond is an archway leading to Temple Church **7**. The griffin statue **8** in the centre of the street marks the site of the original Temple Bar, where the City of Westminster becomes the City of London and the Strand begins.

There's some lovely old buildings along the southern side of the Strand, including the Wig & Pen Club **9** at Nos 229-230, an Art Deco branch of Lloyd's Bank at Nos 222-225 and, at No 216, Thomas Twinings **10**, a teashop operating since 1706. To the north is the extraordinary Royal Courts of Justice **11** built in 1874, where civil (eg, libel) cases are heard. In the middle of the road is St Clement Danes **12** where at 9am, noon, 3pm or 6pm the bells chime 'Oranges and Lemons'. Farther west is St Mary-le-Strand **13**; the elegant building to the south-west is Somerset House **14**, which houses three important museums: the Courtauld Gallery, the Gilbert Collection and the Hermitage Rooms.

**distance** 1.4 miles (2.2km)
**duration** 2½hrs
▶ **start** ⊖ Blackfriars or St Paul's
● **end** ⊖ Embankment or
Temple (closed Sun)

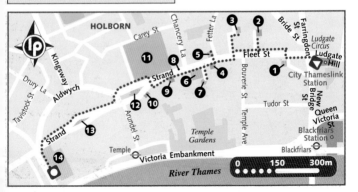

## East End Amble

Emerging from the tube, have a look at the restored Liverpool Street train station ❶ and the modern Broadgate Centre ❷. Cross the road and walk north, turning east into Folgate St where you'll pass the quirky Dennis Severs' House ❸. Continue east and turn south (right) into Commercial St. On the right is the covered Spitalfields Market ❹ and opposite is Christ Church, Spitalfields ❺, built by Nicholas Hawksmoor in 1729.

Dennis Severs' House (p. 46)
Spitalfields Market (p. 61)
Christ Church, Spitalfields (p. 41)
Brick Lane (p. 35)

Continue east along Fournier St, admiring the fine Georgian houses. At the Brick Lane end is the New French Church ❻, built for French Huguenot weavers in 1743; in 1899 the church became a synagogue and in 1975 a mosque.

Brick Lane ❼ is a heady mix of curry houses and shops selling bright fabrics, spices and Islamic religious items. For a quick bite to eat, stop in at the *Brick Lane Beigel*

*Experiencing Brick Lane's cultural diversity*

*Bake* (☎ 7729 0616) at No 159 for some of the best and cheapest filled bagels in town. Walk south along Brick Lane and turn east (left) into Whitechapel High St, which becomes Whitechapel Rd. At Nos 32-34 is the Whitechapel Bell Foundry ❽ (☎ 7247 2599), where Big Ben and the Liberty Bell were cast (pre-booked tour Saturday 10am; £8).

At Cambridge Heath Rd's corner is the Blind Beggar pub ❾, where Ronnie Kray shot George Cornell in 1966 in a turf war over control of the East End's organised crime.

**distance** 1½ miles (2.5km)
**duration** 2hrs
▶ **start** ⊖ Liverpool Street
● **end** ⊖ Whitechapel

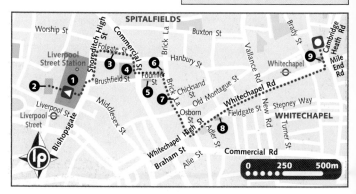

# EXCURSIONS

## Brighton (1, E4)

Brighton, with its mix of seediness and sophistication, is London's favourite seaside resort. The town's popularity dates from the mid-1780s when the dissolute, music-loving Prince Regent (later King George IV) built his outrageous summer palace, the **Royal Pavilion**, here for lavish parties by the sea. Brighton still has some of the hottest clubs and venues outside London as well as a vibrant student population, excellent shopping, a thriving arts scene and countless restaurants, pubs and cafes.

The Royal Pavilion is an extraordinary folly – Indian palace on the outside and over-the-top *chinoiserie* within. Visit the Long Gallery, Banqueting Room, South Galleries, the superb Great Kitchen and the restored Music Room; do not miss Rex Whistler's irreverent 1944 painting *HRH The Prince Regent Awakening the Spirit of Brighton*.

### INFORMATION

*51 miles (82km) south of London*

🚆 Victoria (40 fast trains daily; 50mins); King's Cross, Blackfriars & London Bridge (1hr)

🚌 National Express (hrly; 1hr 50mins)

ⓘ TIC (☎ 0906 711 2255, [e] www.visitbrighton.com), 10 Bartholomew Sq; **Royal Pavilion** (☎ 01273-290900), Pavilion Pde 🕘 Mon-Sun 10am-6pm (till 5pm Oct-May) $ £5.20/ 3.75/3.20/13.60 a/s&st/c/f ♿ fair

🍴 Terre à Terre (☎ 01273-729051), 71 East St

Bryn Thomas

*The Royal Pavilion's magical Indian exterior, Brighton*

# Cambridge  (1, A5)

The university at Cambridge was founded in the 13th century, several decades later than Oxford. There is fierce rivalry between the two cities and universities, and an ongoing debate over which is the best and most beautiful. If you have the time, you should visit both. If you've only time for one and the major colleges (St John's, Trinity, King's etc) are open, choose Cambridge. Oxford draws more tourists and can seem more like a provincial city with a university; Cambridge's architectural treasure house makes it the foremost English university town. There are three eight-week academic terms: Michaelmas (October to December), Lent(mid-January to mid-March) and Easter (mid-April to mid-June).

The **Fitzwilliam Museum** has

## INFORMATION

*54 miles (87km) north of London*

- King's Cross (every 30mins; 1hr); Liverpool Street (every 30mins; 55mins)
- National Express (hrly; 2hrs)
- ⓘ TIC (☎ 01223-322640, e www.cambridge.gov.uk), Wheeler St near Market Sq; 2hr guided tours ⏰ Mon-Sun 1.30pm Ⓢ £7/4 a/c; **Fitzwilliam Museum** (☎ 01223-332923 e www.fitzmuseum.cam .ac.uk), Trumpington St ⏰ Tues-Sat 10am-5pm, Sun 2.15-5pm Ⓢ free ♿ good
- ✖ Browns (☎ 01223-461655), 23 Trumpington St

### Taking a punt

Be sure to try your hand at that favourite of Cambridge pastimes: punting along the gentle River Cam. Boats can be hired from Trinity Punts (☎ 01223-338483), Garret Hostel Lane (£6/hr, £25 deposit) or from Scudamore's (☎ 01223-359750), Grant Place (£12/hr, £60 deposit).

an important collection of ancient Egyptian sarcophagi and Greek and Roman art in its lower galleries and a wide range of paintings (including the Impressionists) upstairs.

*The glorius King's College Chapel, Cambridge University*

## Hampton Court Palace (1, B4)

In 1515 Cardinal Thomas Wolsey built a grand palace but was later forced to hand it over to Henry VIII. Henry set to work expanding it, adding the Great Hall, the Chapel and the sprawling kitchens. By 1540 this was one of the grandest palaces in Europe. In the late 17th century, Christopher Wren built extensions.

Stairs inside Anne Boleyn's Gateway lead up to Henry VIII's State Apartments and the Great Hall. Off the Great Watching Chamber is the Haunted Gallery, visited frequently, they say, by Henry's fifth wife, Catherine Howard. The Tudor Kitchens have been fitted out to look as they might have done in Henry's day, and the King's Apartments have been extensively restored.

Outside there are the wonderful Privy Gardens, and the famous half-a-mile-long (1km) hornbeam and yew maze planted in 1690.

**INFORMATION**

*9 miles (15km) west of London*

🚆 Waterloo (every 30mins)

⛴ Westminster Pier (☎ 7930 4721; [e] www.wpsa.co.uk; 3 daily Apr-Sept/Oct, 3½hrs)

☎ 8781 9500

[e] www.hrp.org.uk

🕒 Mon 10.15am-6pm, Tues-Sun 9.30am-6pm (late Oct–mid-March to 4.30pm)

$ £10.80/8.50/7.20/32.30 a/s&st/c/f; Privy Gardens £2.50/1.30 a/c; maze £2.50/1.60 a/c

## Windsor Castle (1, B3)

Standing on chalk bluffs overlooking the Thames, Windsor Castle has been home to British royalty for over 900 years and is one of the greatest surviving medieval castles. Prime attractions are **St George's Chapel**, a fine example of late Gothic architecture and packed with the tombs of royalty (including those of George III and Henry VIII), and the **State Apartments**, now restored after having been partially destroyed by fire in 1992. Windsor Castle is the weekend residence of the royal family and parts of the castle may be closed off at that time, including St George's Chapel on Sunday.

In May and June, weather (and other events) permitting, the changing of the guard takes place Monday to Saturday at 11am (alternate days Monday to Saturday the rest of the year).

**INFORMATION**

*23 miles (37km) west of London*

🚆 Waterloo to Riverside Station (every 30mins; 55mins), Paddington to Windsor Central Station (hrly; 30mins)

🚌 Green Line bus (5-10 daily; 1hr)

☎ 01753-869898, 01753-831118 (opening times)

[e] www.the-royal-collection.org.uk

ⓘ TIC (☎ 01753-743900, [e] www.windsor.gov.uk), 24 High St

🕒 Mon-Sun 9.45am-5.15pm (Nov-Feb to 4.15pm)

$ £11/9/5.50/27.50 a/s/c/f (£5.50/4.50/2.70/13.70 when State Apartments closed)

🍴 Francesco's (☎ 01753-863773), 53 Peascod St

# ORGANISED TOURS

## TOUR GUIDES

**Association of Professional Tourist Guides**
*La crème de la crème* of British guides are the 900 knowledgeable members of the APTG (Blue Badge Guides), who study for two years and sit both written and practical examinations before being awarded the coveted 'Blue Badge'. You can decide where you want to go and for how long, or take advice from them. They're not cheap but it can be affordable if there's a number of you.
**☎ 7403 2962 [e] www.touristguides.org.uk $ £85/128 half/full day (English), £97/154 (other language)**

## BICYCLE TOURS

**London Bicycle Tour Company** (3, G9)
Onn offer are three-hour cycle tours of the East End (Globe Theatre, Tower Bridge, Tobacco Dock, the East End proper, the City and St Paul's Cathedral) and West End (Houses of Parliament, Lambeth Palace, Kensington and Chelsea, the Royal Albert Hall, Buckingham Palace, St James's, Trafalgar Square and Covent Garden); often the group elects a different routing altogether in consultation with the leader.
**✉ 1a Gabriel's Wharf, 56 Upper Ground SE1 ☎ 7928 6838 [e] www.londonbicycle.com 🕐 East Tour Sat 2pm, Royal West Tour Sun 2pm $ £11.95 (inc. bike)**

## BUS TOURS

**Original London Sightseeing Tour**
The best known of many London sightseeing bus companies, this one hits the main sights in double-decker buses, allowing you to hop on and off along the way and reboard the next bus. Convenient starting points are: Trafalgar Sq; in front of Baker Street tube station next to Madame Tussaud's; on Haymarket south-east of Piccadilly Circus; Marble Arch (Speakers' Corner); and in Grosvenor Gardens opposite Victoria Station.
**☎ 8877 1722 [e] www.theoriginaltour.com 🕐 9am-7/8pm, winter 9/9.30am-5/6pm $ £14/7.50 a/c**

## WATER TOURS

**City Cruises** (3, H7)
City Cruises operates a year-round ferry service from Westminster Pier to Tower Pier and Tower Pier to Greenwich in a continuous loop that allows passengers to jump on and jump off at various stops. Boats depart every 20-40mins, with later departures in summer and fewer sailings in winter.
**✉ Westminster Pier SW1 ☎ 7740 0400 [e] www.citycruises.com 🕐 10/10.30am-5/6pm (June-Aug later, Nov-Mar fewer sailings) $ £7.50/3.75/19.50 a/c/f**

**Westminster Passenger Services Association** (3, H7)
WPSA river boats link central London with the Royal Botanic Gardens at Kew (1½hrs) and Hampton Court Palace (3½hrs) generally from late March/April to September/October. Phone for exact schedules.
**✉ Westminster Pier SW1 ☎ 7930 4721 [e] www.wpsa.co.uk 🕐 Kew (via Putney): late Mar-Sept/Oct 10.15am-2pm**

### Guided Walks

*Time Out*'s 'Around Town: Listings' section lists what's on offer. Some popular themes are The Beatles' Magical Mystery Tour, Jewish London and, inevitably, a tour in the footsteps of Jack the Ripper through Whitechapel. Walks take about 2hrs and cost around £5/4 a/s&st.

These companies offer guided walks:

| | |
|---|---|
| **Capital Walks** | ☎ 8650 7640 |
| **Cityguide Walks** | ☎ 01895-675389 |
| **Discover London on Foot** | ☎ 01494-888520, [e] www.tourlondon.com |
| **Historical Tours** | ☎ 8668 4019 |
| **Original London Walks** | ☎ 7624 3978; [e] www.walks.com |
| **Ray's Route of Rock** | ☎ 7733 5347 |

**(5 sailings); Hampton Court Palace: Apr-Sept/Oct 10.30am, 11.15am, noon $ to/from Kew: £7/6/3 a/s/c single, £11/9/5 return; Hampton Court Palace: £10/8/4 single, £14/11/7 return**

## Not Quite Venice

London's 40 miles (65km) of inner-city canals, most of them constructed for industry in the early 19th century, are being given a new lease of life as leisure resources. The 2½-mile-long (4km) Regent's Canal, looping around north London from Little Venice in Maida Vale to Camden Lock, passing near London Zoo and Regent's Park, is a popular route for boating tour groups. British Waterways (☎ 7286 6101; [e] www.british-waterways.co.uk) has a free *Explore London's Canals* pamphlet that lists six towpath walks.

**Jenny Wren** (4, C3)
Jenny Wren offers dinner and Sunday lunch cruises along Regent's Canal aboard *My Fair Lady*. The dates of the dinner cruise are fixed each week; call ahead for information and bookings.
**✉ Waterside Café, 250 Camden High St NW1 ☎ 7485 4433 🕘 dinner Tues-Sat 8-11pm, Sun lunch 12.30-3.30pm $ dinner cruise £21.95, Sun lunch cruise £18.95**

**London Waterbus Company** (4, C3)
The London Waterbus Company runs 90-minute trips on Regent's Canal in an enclosed canal barge between Camden Lock and Little Venice, passing through Regent's Park and London Zoo along the way.
**✉ Middle Yard, Camden Lock NW1 ☎ 7482 2660 (information), 7482 2550 (bookings) 🕘 Apr-Oct: Mon-Sun 10am-5pm (hrly, every 30mins Sun); Nov-Mar: weekends only 10am-3/4pm (hrly) $ £4.20/2.80 a/c single, £5.60/3.60 return**

## AIR TOURS

**Cabair Helicopters**
**(1, A4)** If you can stump up the dosh, Cabair Helicopters offers 30-minute helicopter 'flight-seeing' tours over London every Sunday.
**✉ Elstree Aerodrome, Borehamwood, Herts ☎ 8953 4411 [e] www.cabair.com $ £125**

## DAY TRIPS

**Adventure Travel Centre** (2, H3)
Organises Sunday coach trips specifically aimed at (but not limited to) the Australasian market, with trips usually taking in two destinations (eg, Oxford and Blenheim Palace or Leeds Castle and Canterbury). Longer festival trips (eg, Ladies Day at Ascot, Edinburgh Tattoo) cost from £169 for four days.
**✉ 131 Earl's Court Rd SW5 ☎ 7370 4555 [e] www.topdecktravel.co.uk 🕘 Sun 8.30am-6pm $ £12**

**Astral Tours**
Mini-coach tours cover one or several of the following: Bath, the Cotswolds, Oxford, Salisbury, Stonehenge, Avebury, Glastonbury and Stratford-upon-Avon. Students and YHA/HI members get a 20% discount on some tours and everyone gets a 5% discount if they book online.
**☎ 0700 078 1016 or 0870 902 0908 [e] www.astraltravels.co.uk $ day trip £47-49, inc. all admission fees**

**Golden Tours** (3, K3)
Offers coach excursions with pick-ups from 65 London hotels to a great number of destinations (eg, Windsor, Windsor with Hampton Court Gardens, Oxford, Stratford, Bath and Stonehenge etc).
**✉ 4 Fountain Sq, 123-151 Buckingham Palace Rd SW1 ☎ 7233 7030 [e] www.goldentours.co.uk $ half-day trip to Windsor & Runnymede £27.50/24 a/c, inc. admission to castle; to Leeds Castle £29.50/25**

Dennis Johnson

*Royal Windsor's castle*

# shopping

London is a mecca for shoppers, and if you can't find it here, it probably doesn't exist. If you're looking for something with a British 'brand' on it, eschew the Union Jack-emblazoned kitsch of **Carnaby St** and **Oxford St** and go for what the Brits themselves know are of good quality, sometimes stylish and always well-made: Dr Marten boots and shoes, Burberry raincoats and umbrellas, tailor-made shirts and suits from **Jermyn St** and **Savile Row**, Royal Doulton china and glassware, costume jewellery (be it for the finger, wrist, nose, eyebrow or navel). London's music stores and, especially, bookshops are celebrated on the street and in literature; many cater for the most obscure of tastes. And the word 'antique' does not always have to be prefaced by 'priceless' – you'll find any number of affordable curios and baubles at London's many markets.

## Shopping Areas

Although most things can be bought throughout London, a trip to the **West End** makes for particularly good shopping. **Covent Garden**, the vegetable market of the West End for 150 years, was redeveloped in the 1980s; the twee shops and stalls inside the old market hall tend to be pricey and tourist-oriented. Luckily the nearby streets, **Neal St** and **Neal's Yard** in particular, remain a happy hunting ground for seekers of designer and/or street clothing and footwear, funky gifts, household goods and natural therapy products.

**Oxford St** can be a great disappointment. Selfridges is up there with Harrods as a place to visit; Peter Jones' sister store, John Lewis, makes the same claim to unbeatable prices; and the flagship Marks & Spencer at the Marble Arch (western) end has its fans. But the farther east you go, the tackier and less interesting it gets. **Regent St**, with Liberty and Hamleys, is much more upmarket. For streetwear **High St Kensington**

### West End Buys

Some streets have particular specialities:

**Cecil Court** – antiquarian bookshops
**Charing Cross Rd** – new and second-hand books
**Denmark St** – musical instruments, sheet music, books about music
**Hanway St** – used records
**St Christopher's Place** – jewellery shops
**Tottenham Court Rd** – electronics and computer shops

Simon Bracken

*An old curiosity bookshop*

and **King's Rd** are good alternatives to Oxford St. Any international designer – from the Italians and French to the Japanese – worth his or her threads has at least one outlet in London, usually on **Sloane St** or **Bond St** or in **Knightsbridge**. In the **City** check out the lovely boutiques along **Bow Lane**, between Cheapside and Cannon St.

# DEPARTMENT STORES

Some London department stores are tourist attractions in their own right; few visitors leave without popping into Harrods and Fortnum & Mason, even if only to browse. And the cult TV series *Absolutely Fabulous* has made Harvey Nichols (or 'Harvey Nicks') another must-see attraction.

**Fortnum & Mason**
(3, G4) All kinds of unusual foodstuffs, along with the famous food hampers, can be purchased from its exotic, old-world food hall. This emporium also has plenty of fashion on its six other floors.
⊠ 181 Piccadilly W1
☎ 7734 8040 ⓔ www.fortnumandmason.co.uk ⊖ Piccadilly Circus
⊕ Mon-Sat 10am-6.30pm

**Harrods** (3, J1)
This celebrated store is truly unique but it does have its down sides: it's always crowded, there are more rules than an army boot camp and it's hard to find what you're looking for. But the toilets are fab, the food halls will make you swoon, and if Harrods hasn't got it, it ain't worth having.
⊠ 87-135 Brompton Rd SW1 ☎ 7730 1234
ⓔ www.harrods.com

⊖ Knightsbridge
⊕ Mon-Sat 10am-7pm

**Harvey Nichols** (3, H1)
The city's temple of high fashion has a great 5th-floor food hall, extravagant perfume and jewellery departments, and all the big names – from Versace to Alexander McQueen.
⊠ 109-125 Knightsbridge SW1 ☎ 7235 5000 ⓔ www.harveynichols.com ⊖ Knightsbridge ⊕ Mon-Tues & Sat 10am-7pm, Wed-Fri 10am-8pm, Sun 12-6pm

**John Lewis** (6, A1)
This London institution, part of the same group as Peter Jones, is the place to know about if you're looking for household goods. John Lewis' motto – 'Never knowingly undersold' – is not just hype; buy something, find it cheaper elsewhere and they'll make up the difference.
⊠ 278-306 Oxford St

W1 ☎ 7629 7711
ⓔ www.johnlewis.co.uk ⊖ Oxford Circus
⊕ Mon-Wed & Fri 9.30am-7pm, Thurs 10am-8pm, Sat 9am-6pm

*Luxuriant Liberty style*

**Liberty** (6, B2)
Almost as unique as Harrods, Liberty was born out of the Arts and Crafts Movement – in Italy Art Nouveau is still called Stile Liberty. It has high fashion, modern furniture, super luxury fabrics and those inimitable Liberty silk scarves.
⊠ 210-220 Regent St W1 ☎ 7734 1234
ⓔ www.liberty-of-london.com ⊖ Oxford Circus ⊕ Mon-Wed 10am-6.30pm, Thurs 10am-8pm, Fri-Sat 10am-7pm, Sun 12-6pm

**Marks & Spencer**
(3, E2) M&S is almost as British as fish and chips, beans on toast and warm beer. It has the full range of fashion goods, but most

## Sales

The biannual sales at London's department stores, when every tourist, London resident *and* their grandmothers seem to be queuing up outside Harrods or some other big shop, take place in January and July.

*Rich colours in Knightsbridge*

people shop here for underwear, well-made affordable clothes and ready-made meals.

✉ **458 Oxford St W1**
☎ **7935 7954** e www .marksandspencer.co.uk
⊖ **Marble Arch** ⊘ **Mon-Fri 9am-8pm, Sat 9am-7pm, Sun 12-6pm**

**Peter Jones** (2, H6)
Due to its posh locale and more well-heeled clientele than sister-store John Lewis, it's been described as the 'best corner shop in Chelsea'.
✉ **Sloane Sq SW1**
☎ **7730 3434** e www .johnlewis.co.uk
⊖ **Sloane Square**

⊘ **Mon-Wed & Fri 9.30am-7pm, Thurs 10am-8pm, Sat 9am-6pm**

**Selfridges** (3, E2)
Arguably the grandest department store on Oxford St, Selfridges boasts some excellent food halls (enter from Orchard St), which are much less confusing, cramped and crowded than the ones at Harrods.
✉ **400 Oxford St W1**
☎ **7629 1234** e www .selfridges.co.uk
⊖ **Bond Street** ⊘ **Mon-Wed 10am-7pm, Thurs-Fri 10am-8pm, Sat 9.30am-7pm, Sun 12-6pm**

### VAT
Value-added tax (VAT) is a 17.5% sales tax levied on most goods (except food, books and children's clothing) and services in the UK. If you're not an EU citizen, it's sometimes possible to get a VAT refund on goods you take home with you. Not all shops participate in the refund scheme, and minimum-purchase conditions vary (normally around £75). Ask for details when making a purchase.

# MARKETS

**Bermondsey** (2, G12)
This is the place to come if you're after 'curios' rather than 'antiques'. The main market on Friday morning takes place outdoors on the square, although adjacent warehouses shelter the more vulnerable furnishings and bric-a-brac and are open throughout the week. Nearby Tower Bridge Rd is another good street to check out.
✉ **Bermondsey Sq, junction of Bermondsey St & Long La SE1**
☎ **7969 1500**
⊖ **Borough, Bermondsey** ⊘ **Fri 5am-1pm**

**Brick Lane** (3, C15)
This market is a lot more fun than the nearby one on Petticoat Lane (p. 60) but the recent revival of Spitalfields Market (p. 61) has left it in the dust. There's a mix of stalls spreading from Brick Lane along Bethnal Green Rd and

selling clothes, fruit and vegetables, household goods, paintings, bric-a-brac and cigarettes imported from the continent.
✉ **Brick La E1**
⊖ **Shoreditch, Aldgate East** ⊘ **Sun 8am-1pm**

**Brixton** (2, K9)
Brixton Market is a cosmopolitan treat that mixes everything from the Body Shop and reggae music to slick Muslim preachers, South American butcher shops and exotic fruits. In Electric Avenue and the covered Granville Arcade you can buy wigs, uncommon foods such as tilapia fish and Ghanaian eggs (really a type of vegetable), unusual spices and homeopathic root cures.
✉ **Reliance & Granville Arcades, Market Row, Electric La & Electric Ave SW9** ⊖ **Brixton** ⊘ **Mon-Tues, Thurs-Sat 8am-6pm & Wed 8am-3pm**

**Camden** (4, C3)
Visit the market at the weekend (especially Sunday), although most days there'll be some stalls open. It's massive and comprises several sections, including Camden Canal Market which sells bric-a-brac from around the world; Camden Market itself, which houses stalls for fashion, clothing and jewellery; Camden Lock Market, with ceramics, furniture, oriental rugs, musical instruments and designer clothes; and the Stables, the northernmost part of the market, with antiques, Asian artefacts, rugs and carpets, pine furniture, and 1950s and 60s clothing.
✉ **Camden High St & Chalk Farm Rd NW1**
⊖ **Camden Town** ⊘ **Sat-Sun 10am-6pm**

**Covent Garden** (6, C7)
While the shops in the Covent Garden Piazza are open daily, a couple of markets

also take place here. The better one is the Apple Market in the North Hall with quality crafts sold daily. On Monday there's an antiques and bric-a-brac market in Jubilee Hall on the southern side of the Piazza in Jubilee Hall; during the rest of the week it's full of schlock.

✉ Covent Garden

Piazza WC2 ⊖ Covent Garden ☉ Apple Market 9am-5pm; Jubilee Market Mon 9am-3pm, Tues-Sun 9am-5pm

**Greenwich (5, C2)**
This is a great place to look for decorated glass, rugs, prints, wooden toys and other craft items. There's also antiques and curios on Thursday. South of Church St and opposite St Alfege Church, there's the small Village Market Antiques Centre, with the obligatory mix: second-hand clothes, handmade jewellery, plants and household bric-a-brac.

✉ College Approach, King William Walk & Greenwich Church St SE10 ▣ DLR Cutty Sark ☉ Wed & Fri-Sun 9.30am-5.30pm, Thurs 9am-5pm; Antiques Centre: Fri & Sat 10am-5pm, Sun 10am-6pm

**Petticoat Lane**
(3, D15) Petticoat Lane is east London's long-established Sunday market on Middlesex St (the border of the City and White-chapel). These days, it's full of run-of-the-mill trash and tourists lost in a forest of cheap T-shirts and trainers.

✉ Middlesex & Wentworth Sts E1 ⊖ Aldgate, Aldgate East, Liverpool Street ☉ Sun 8am-2pm (Wentworth St only Mon-Fri 9am-2pm)

**Portobello Rd (2, F3)**
After Camden, this is London's most famous (and crowded) weekend street market. Starting at Notting Hill Gate, it wends its way to the Westway flyover in Ladbroke Grove. Antiques, handmade jewellery, paintings and ethnic stuff are concentrated at the Notting Hill Gate end; west to Elgin Crescent and east to Colville Terrace the stalls dip downmarket, selling fruit and vegetables, second-hand clothing, cheap

---

## To Market, to Market

Other interesting markets close to central London are:

**Berwick St** (6, B4; ⊖ Piccadilly Circus, Oxford Circus) – fruit and vegetables

**Billingsgate** (2, E15; ▣ DLR West India Quay) – wholesale fish market

**Borough** (6, G12; ⊖ London Bridge) – general produce, English farm cheeses, specialist sausages, pastries

**Columbia Rd** (3, A15; ⊖ Bethnal Green; ▣ Cambridge Heath, then bus 26, 48 or 55) – flowers, plants

**Leadenhall** (3, E13; ⊖ Bank) – fresh fish, meat, cheese

**Leather Lane** (3, C9; ⊖ Chancery Lane) – cheap videos, tapes and CDs, household goods, clothing

**Ridley Rd** (2, A13; ▣ Dalston Kingsland; ▣ 149 or 242 from Liverpool St) – Afro-Caribbean and Turkish produce and delicacies

**Roman Rd** (2, C15; ⊖ Mile End; ▣ 8 or 277) – discount clothes

**Smithfield** (3, D10; ⊖ Farringdon) – last surviving meat market in central London

*The London Market Guide* (Metro Publications; £5.99) by Andrew Richard Kershman and Ally Ireson has the lowdown on smaller local markets and ones farther afield (eg, those in Shepherd's Bush, Swiss Cottage, Walthamstow and Wembley).

*British paraphernalia*

Neil Setchfield

household goods and general junk. Though a few shops and stalls open daily, the busiest days for clothing and bric-a-brac are Friday, Saturday and Sunday. There's also an antiques market Saturday and a flea market on Portobello Green Sunday morning.
✉ **Portobello Rd W10**
✈ **Notting Hill Gate, Ladbroke Grove,**

**Westbourne Park**
🕐 **Mon-Wed 8am-6pm, Thurs 9am-1pm, Fri 7am-7pm, Sat 6am-5pm, Sun 6am-2pm**

**Spitalfields** (3, C15)
Housed in a huge Victorian covered warehouse, Spitalfields has a great mix of arts and crafts, organic fruit and veg, stylish new and retro clothes, and second-hand books, with interesting ethnic shops ringing the central area.
Most of the shops in the market open weekdays as well (10.30am-5pm) and there's an organic produce market on Friday.
✉ **Commercial St E1**
✈ **Liverpool Street, Shoreditch** 🕐 **Sun 9.30am-5.30pm**

# ANTIQUES

Antique hunters may find something worthwhile at the Saturday antiques market along Portobello Rd, but better pickings are to be had at Camden Passage and Bermondsey Market.

**Antiquarius Antiques Centre** (2, J6)
This centre is packed with 120 stalls selling everything from top hats and ancient corkscrews to old luggage and jewellery. It's definitely worth a rummage.
✉ **131-141 King's Rd SW3** ☎ **7351 5353**
✈ **Sloane Square**
🕐 **Mon-Sat 10am-6pm**

**Camden Passage**
(2, C10) This cavern with four arcades full of antique shops and stalls is in Islington and has nothing to do with Camden Market. Stalls sell pretty much everything to which the moniker 'antique' or 'curio' could reasonably be applied, and the stallholders know their stuff, so real bargains are a rarity.
✉ **Upper St & Essex Rd N1** ☎ **7359 0190**
✈ **Angel** 🕐 **Wed 7.30am-2pm, Sat 8am-4pm**

**LASSCo** (3, B14)
LASSCo is a recycler's heaven, with everything from slate tiles and oak floorboards to vast marble fireplaces and

garden follies – along with much smaller curios – available. Its location, in a disused church, is worth the trip alone.
✉ **St Michael's Church, Mark St EC2** ☎ **7749 9944** ✉ **www.lassco.co.uk** ✈ **Old Street** 🕐 **Mon & Wed-Sat 10am-5pm, Tues 10am-8pm**

**London Silver Vaults**
(3, D9) The 40 subterranean shops in Chancery House, collectively known as the London Silver Vaults, is the largest collection of silver under on roof in the world. The shops sell anything in metal – from jewellery and picture frames to candelabra and tea services for 12.
✉ **53-63 Chancery La WC2** ☎ **7242 3844**
✈ **Chancery Lane**
🕐 **Mon-Fri 9am 5.30pm, Sat 9am-1pm**

## Once, Twice, SOLD!
Fancy a spot of upmarket shopping without the predictability of fixed price tags? Pop into one of London's auction houses, those household-name powerhouses where Van Goghs routinely change hands for zillions of pounds, but where sales of more affordable ephemera also take place. The best-known ones include:

**Bonhams** (Montpelier St SW7; 2, G6; ☎ 7393 3900; ✉ www.bonhams.com; ✈ Knightsbridge)
**Christie's** (8 King St SW1; 6, E3; ☎ 7839 9060; ✉ www.christies.com; ✈ Green Park, Piccadilly Circus)
**Phillips** (101 New Bond St W1; 6, B1; ☎ 7629 6602; ✉ www.phillips-auctions.com; ✈ Bond St)
**Sotheby's** (34-35 New Bond St W1; 6, C2; ☎ 7293 5000; ✉ www.sothebys.com; ✈ Bond St)

# CLOTHING & ACCESSORIES

**Agent Provocateur**
(6, B4) For women's lingerie to die for (or over, or in), check out this decidedly window-shoppable place.
✉ 6 Broadwick St W1
☎ 7439 0229 e www
.agentprovocateur
.com ⊖ Oxford Circus
🕐 Mon-Sat 11am-7pm

**Aquascutum** (6, D3)
This bastion of British design is moving ahead but is still the place for retro-inspired pea jackets and storm coats.
✉ 100 Regent St W1
☎ 7675 8200 e www
.aquascutum.co.uk
⊖ Piccadilly Circus
🕐 Mon-Wed & Fri-Sat 10am-6.30pm, Thurs 10am-7pm, Sun 12-5pm

**Betty Jackson** (2, H5)
Fashionable – but not overly so – linen, suede and knit pieces for women.
✉ 311 Brompton Rd SW3 ☎ 7589 7884
⊖ South Kensington
🕐 Mon-Fri 10am-
6.30pm, Sat 10am-6pm, Sun 12-5pm

**Burberry** (6, C2)
Head here for that most English of articles of clothing – the macintosh – in its distinctive tartan pattern.
✉ 21-23 New Bond St SW1 ☎ 7839 5222
⊖ Bond Street, Oxford Circus 🕐 Mon-Sat 10am-7pm, Sun 12-6pm

**French Connection UK**
(3, E3) FCUK, the high-street chain with the in-your-face name, still leads in style and quality in the street-chic department.
✉ 396 Oxford St W1
☎ 7629 7766 e www
.frenchconnection.com
⊖ Bond Street
🕐 Mon-Wed & Fri 10am-8pm, Thurs 10am-9pm, Sat 10am-7pm, Sun 12-6pm

**High Jinks** (6, B6)
Large streetwear emporium crammed with street fashion

by struggling young designers, who are more than a little keen to sell their imaginative glad rags.
✉ Thomas Neal Centre, Earlham St WC2 ☎ 7240 5580
e www.high-jinks
.com ⊖ Covent Garden
🕐 Mon-Sat 10am-7pm, Sun 12-6pm

**James Smith & Sons**
(6, A6) No-one, but no-one, makes and stocks umbrellas (along with canes and walking sticks) like James Smith & Sons; the shop's mirrored exterior is a museum piece.
✉ 53 New Oxford St WC1 ☎ 7836 4731
e www.james-smith
.co.uk ⊖ Holborn, Tottenham Court Road
🕐 Mon-Fri 9.30am-5.25pm, Sat 10am-5.25pm

**Nicole Farhi** (6, D2)
Smart and classic Farhi knitwear, suits and dresses are snapped up by women for the beautiful fabrics used and the attention given to comfort. The designer has also extended her line of menswear.
✉ 158 New Bond St W1
☎ 7499 8368
⊖ Bond Street
🕐 Mon-Wed & Fri 10am-6pm, Thurs 10am-7pm, Sat 10am-6.30pm

**Paul Smith** (6, C7)
Cleverly cut and very wearable men's and women's lines have made the recently knighted Smith one of the most sought after Brit designers.
✉ 40-44 Floral St WC2
☎ 7379 7133 e www
.paulsmith.co.uk

## Britpack

Watch out for classic British designers such as Alexander McQueen (who also does a cool range of sunglasses), Amanda Wakeley, Vivienne Westwood, Paul Smith and Nicole Farhi, as well as newcomers Roland Mouret, Scott Henshall, Tracey Mulligan and Liza Bruce, who mix formal design with hip streetwear. The following designer shops are worth a browse, even if you can't afford their fripperies:

**Alexander McQueen** (47 Conduit St W1; 6, C2; ☎ 7734 2340; ⊖ Oxford Circus, Piccadilly Circus)
**Amanda Wakeley** (80 Fulham Rd SW3; 2, H5; ☎ 7590 9105; ⊖ South Kensington)
**Tomasz Starewski** (14 Stanhope Mews West SW7; 2, H4; ☎ 7244 6138; ⊖ Gloucester Road)

⊖ Covent Garden ⏲ Mon-Wed & Fri 10.30am-6.30pm, Thurs 10.30am-7pm, Sat 10am-6.30, Sun 1-5pm

**Ralph Lauren** (6, D2)
Simple but elegant classic English dresses, tunics and tops for women; high-quality shirts, trousers and jumpers for men.
⊠ 1 New Bond St W1
☎ 7535 4600 **e** www .ralphlauren.com ⊖ Piccadilly Circus, Green Park ⏲ Mon-Thurs & Fri-Sat 10am-6pm

**Rigby & Peller** (3, J1)
Not a purveyor of lingerie, thank you, but a corsetière, R&P's makes Her Maj's brassieres. Both off-the-peg and bespoke bras,

corsets and swimwear are available.
⊠ 2 Hans Rd SW3
☎ 7589 9293 **e** www .rigbyandpeller.com ⊖ Knightsbridge ⏲ Mon-Tues & Thurs-Sat 10am-6pm, Wed 10am-7pm

**Vivienne Westwood** (3, E3) Longevity has not tamed the unpredictable offerings of punk's grand-mother, who still shocks, stocks and sells.
⊠ 6 Davies St W1
☎ 7629 3757 ⊖ Bond Street ⏲ Mon-Wed & Fri-Sat 10am-6pm, Thurs 10am-7pm

**Zara** (6, C3)
This is where to come for fashionable throwaways that are here today and

gone tomorrow.
⊠ 118 Regent St W1
☎ 7534 9500 **e** www .zara.com ⊖ Piccadilly Circus, Oxford Circus ⏲ Mon-Wed & Fri-Sat 10am-7pm, Thurs 10am-8pm, Sun 12-6pm

Burberry, founded in 1856

# JEWELLERY

**ec one** (3, B9)
Some 30 different design-ers sell their cutting-edge contemporary creations here. One-off commissions are available.
⊠ 41 Exmouth Market EC1 ☎ 7713 6185
**e** www.econe.co.uk ⊖ Farringdon, Angel ⏲ Mon-Fri 10am-6pm, Sat 10.30am-5.30pm

**House of Mouawad** (6, D2) This palace of opu-lence may have been around for well over a century but it's taken the stars forever to discover the 'secret' (recently spotted fingering baubles: Nicole 'Nickers' Kidman and Robbie 'The Bloke from Stoke' Williams).
⊠ 9 New Bond St W1
☎ 7495 4951 **e** www .mouawad.com
⊖ Green Park ⏲ Mon-Sat 10am-5.30pm

## Crowning Jewels

For common garden-variety jewellery, try any of the stalls in the main-line train stations or the markets, though Portobello Green in Portobello Rd Market is home to some cutting-edge jewellery designers. If it's classic settings and unmounted stones you're after, stroll along Hatton Garden EC1 (3, D9; ⊖ Chancery Lane); it's chock-a-block with gold, diamond and jew-ellery shops.

For precious stones head to Mappin & Webb

**Mappin & Webb** (6, C3) For jewellery you'd need to win the lottery to buy, head to this fine shop in business since 1774.
⊠ 170 Regent St W1

☎ 7734 3801 **e** www .mappin-and-web.co.uk ⊖ Oxford Circus, Picca-dilly Circus ⏲ Mon-Wed & Fri-Sat 10am-6pm, Thurs 10am-7pm

# DESIGN, ARTS & CRAFTS

### Botanicals (6, A2)

This wonderful and spacious shop sells handmade organic Czech products – from candles and soaps to herbal vinegars and teas.

✉ 12 Great Portland St W1 ☎ 7637 1610
e www.botanicus.cz
⊖ Oxford Circus
🕓 Mon-Wed & Sat 10am-7pm, Thurs-Fri 8.30am-7pm

### Gosh! (3, D6)

Try this place for comics, cartoons and playing cards with everything imaginable on the reverse.

✉ 39 Great Russell St WC1 ☎ 7636 1011
⊖ Tottenham Court Road 🕓 Sat-Wed

10am-6pm, Thurs-Fri 10am-7pm

### Kitschen Sync (6, B6)

For something really unusual, head for the shop with the cringey name selling 'trashy trinkets' (their words) and groovy retro kitchenware such as zigzag-shaped brooms, shocking-pink kettles and polka-dot plastic chairs.

✉ 7 Earlham St WC2 ☎ 7497 5129 e www .kitchensync.com
⊖ Covent Garden
🕓 Mon-Fri 11am-7pm, Sat 11am-6pm

### Papier Marché

(6, B10) Located in the Clerkenwell Visitors

Centre, this is the place to come for all manner of birds and animals made out of papiermâché.

✉ 53 Clerkenwell Close EC1 ☎ 7251 6311 ⊖ Farringdon
🕓 Mon-Sat 11am-6pm

### Royal Doulton (6, C3)

Head here for classic English bone china and cut glassware.

✉ 154 Regent St W1 ☎ 7734 3184
e www.royal-doulton .com ⊖ Piccadilly Circus 🕓 Mon-Wed & Fri-Sat 10am-6pm, Thurs 10am-7pm, Sun 11am-5pm

# FOOD & DRINK

Run-of-the-mill food shops are ten a penny all over London, but the food halls at Harrods, Selfridges and Fortnum & Mason are attractions in themselves. It's also worth tracking down some of the more specialist stores for savoury and sweet treats.

## Saying Cheese

While having nowhere near the reputation of the French variety, British cheese has its moments in the hard varieties such as Cheddar and Cheshire and the semi-soft cheeses such as Wensleydale and Stilton. Some of the better cheese shops include:

**Neal's Yard Dairy** (17 Shorts Gardens WC2; 6, B6; ☎ 7240 5700; ⊖ Covent Garden) – has a good selection of better (and more esoteric) British cheeses
**Paxton & Whitfield** (93 Jermyn St SW1; 6, E4; ☎ 7930 0259; ⊖ Piccadilly Circus) – London's oldest cheesemonger (1797) claims to stock 200 different varieties and specialises in English hard cheese
**International Cheese Centre** (3b West Mall, Liverpool Street Station EC2; 3, D14; ☎ 7628 6637; ⊖ Liverpool Street) – offers hundreds of varieties, including vegetarian and organic cheeses

### Algerian Coffee Stores (6, B5)

This is *the* place to go to buy all sorts of teas and coffees, including Maragogype (aka the Elephant Bean), the biggest coffee bean in the world.

✉ 52 Old Compton St W1 ☎ 7437 2480
e www.algcoffee.co .uk ⊖ Leicester Square
🕓 Mon-Sat 9am-7pm

### Gerry's (6, B4)

This place stocks a frightening array of alcohol garnered from far-flung parts, including Peruvian *pisco*, Polish *zubrówka* (vodka flavoured with bisongrass), Stolichnaya Razberi and 70% absinthe.

✉ **74 Old Compton Rd W1** ☎ 7734 4215 ⊖ Leicester Square ⏲ Mon-Fri 9am-6.30pm, Sat 9am-5.30pm

**Rococo** (2, J5)
Chocoholics will have a gobble-fest in this Chelsea shop, offering everything from lowly British Cadbury (a 'chocolate food' as far as we're concerned) to Belgian Godiva and French Valrhona cooking chocolate.
✉ **321 King's Rd SW3** ☎ 7352 5857 e www .rococochocolates.com ⊖ Sloane Square ⏲ Mon-Fri 9.30am-6pm, Sat 9.30am-5pm

**Simply Sausages** (3, D10) This is a great place to stock up for a barbecue. Among the many sausages on sale are ones made with duck, apricots and oranges as well as Thai, beef and Guinness and vegetarian mushroom and tarragon sausages.
✉ **341 Central Markets, Smithfield Market, cnr Charterhouse & Farringdon Sts** ☎ 7329 3227 ⊖ Farringdon ⏲ Mon-Fri 8am-6pm, Sat 9am-3pm

**The Spice Shop** (2, E3)
This shop has a heady selection of spices, herbs and aromatic essential oils.
✉ **1 Blenheim Crescent W11** ☎ 7221 4448 e www.thespice shop.co.uk ⊖ Ladbroke Grove ⏲ Mon-Sat 9.30am-6pm, Sun 11am-5pm

**The Tea House** (6, B7)
This place has a great range of teas and tisanes plus pots to brew them in.
✉ **15a Neal St WC2** ☎ 7240 7539 ⊖ Covent Garden ⏲ Mon-Sat 10am-7pm, Sun 12-6pm

*Time for a cuppa?*

# MUSIC

The West End has several mega-sized music shops with the largest collections of CDs and tapes in London, including the following (open till at least 9pm Monday to Saturday and 6pm Sunday): **HMV Records** (150 Oxford St W1; 6, A3; ☎ 7631 3423; ⊖ Oxford Circus); **Tower Records** (1 Piccadilly Circus W1; 6, D4; ☎ 7439 2500; ⊖ Piccadilly Circus); and **Virgin Megastore** (14-30 Oxford St W1; 6, A5; ☎ 7631 1234; ⊖ Tottenham Court Road).

There's also a number of smaller shops selling used records in Denmark and Hanway Sts.

**Black Market Records** (6, B4) This is where DJ wannabes go when looking for club dance music.
✉ **25 D'Arblay St W1** ☎ 7437 0478 e www .blackmarket.co.uk ⊖ Oxford Circus ⏲ Mon 12-7pm, Tues-Sat 11am-7pm

**Honest Jon's** (2, E2)
Honest Jon's two adjoining shops stock jazz, soul and reggae.
✉ **276 & 278 Portobello Rd W10** ☎ 8969 9822 e www.honestjons.co .uk ⊖ Ladbroke Grove ⏲ Mon-Sat 10am-6pm, Sun 11am-5pm

**Mole Jazz** (3, A7)
Two floors of vinyl, tapes and CDs – probably the best shop for jazz in London.
✉ **311 Gray's Inn Rd WC1** ☎ 7278 8623 e www.molejazz .com ⊖ King's Cross St Pancras ⏲ Mon-Thurs & Sat 10am-6pm, Fri 10am-8pm

**On the Beat** (6, A5)
The place for the serious record collector; mostly retro (60s and 70s) with helpful staff.
✉ **22 Hanway St W1** ☎ 7637 8934

⊖ Tottenham Court Road ⊘ Mon-Sat 11am-7pm

**Ray's Jazz Shop**
(6, A6) Ray's has both rare and recent jazz, and the staff are helpful and knowledgeable.
✉ 180 Shaftesbury Ave WC2 ☎ 7240 3969 ⊖ Tottenham Court Road ⊘ Mon-Sat 10am-6.30pm, Sun 2pm-5.30pm

**Reckless Records**
(6, B4) These two shops are where to come for second-hand soul, punk and new dance music.
✉ 26 & 30 Berwick St W1 ☎ 7437 4271

e www.reckless.co.uk
⊖ Oxford Circus
⊘ 10am-7pm

**Rough Trade** (2, E3)
This famous punk music stockist does indie better than most.
✉ 130 Talbot Rd W11 ☎ 7229 8541 e www .roughtrade.com ⊖ Ladbroke Grove, Notting Hill Gate ⊘ Mon-Sat 10.30am-6.30pm, Sun 1pm-5pm

In a spin at Reckless Records

# BOOKS

For those who read the book or saw the movie *84 Charing Cross Rd*, the road in question will need no introduction; this is where to go when you want reading material old or new. But it certainly isn't the only place to find general or specialist bookshops.

**Borders** (6, A3)
This branch of the big American chain close to Oxford Circus has four floors of books, magazines and newspapers from around the world and CDs, tapes and DVDs.
✉ 203 Oxford St W1 ☎ 7292 1600 e www .bordersstores.com ⊖ Oxford Circus ⊘ Mon-Sat 9am-11pm, Sun 12-6pm

**Foyle's** (6, B5)
Foyle's is the biggest and by far the messiest and most confusing bookshop in London, but it often stocks titles you may not find elsewhere.
✉ 113-119 Charing Cross Rd WC2 ☎ 7437 5660 e www.foyles

.co.uk ⊖ Tottenham Court Road ⊘ Mon-Sat 9.30am-7.30pm, Sun 12-6pm

**Waterstone's** (6, A5)
The Waterstone's chain's many stores are well stocked, and the helpful staff are knowledgeable. There's a mega-branch, Europe's biggest bookstore, at 203-206 Piccadilly (6, D4).
✉ 121 Charing Cross Rd WC2 ☎ 7434 4291 e waterstones.co.uk ⊖ Tottenham Court Road ⊘ Mon-Sat 9.30am-8pm, Sun 12-6pm

**Books for Cooks**
(2, E2) This place has an enormous collection of

cookery books; there's even a small cafe attached where you can sample some of the recipes from the books.
✉ 4 Blenheim Crescent W11 ☎ 7221 1992 e www.booksfor cooks.com ⊖ Ladbroke Grove ⊘ Mon-Sat 10am-6pm

**Garden Books** (2, E2)
This bookshop, on the same street as Books for Cooks and the seminal Travel Bookshop, is where to head for books on gardening.
✉ 11 Blenheim Crescent W11 ☎ 7278 7654 ⊖ Ladbroke Grove ⊘ Mon-Sat 9am-6pm

**Gay's the Word**
(3, B7) This shop stocks guides and literature for, by and about gay men and women.
✉ **66 Marchmont St WC1** ☎ **7278 7654**
**e** www.gaysthe word.co.uk
⊖ **Russell Square**
🕐 Mon-Sat 10am-6.30pm, Sun 2-6pm

*Start your journey with a trip to a travel bookshop.*

**Grant & Cutler** (6, B3)
This is positively the best – *n'est-ce pas?* – foreign-language bookshop in London, with books in or about everything from Arabic to Zulu.
✉ **55-57 Great Marlborough St W1**
☎ **7734 2012** **e** www.grantandcutler.com
⊖ **Oxford Circus**
🕐 Mon-Wed & Fri-Sat 9am-6pm, Thurs 9am-7pm

**Helter Skelter** (6, A6)
This excellent store with very helpful staff specialises in books about popular music.
✉ **4 Denmark St WC2** ☎ **7836 1151**
**e** www.skelter.demon.co.uk ⊖ **Oxford Circus**
🕐 Mon-Fri 10am-7pm, Sat 10am-6pm

**Murder One** (6, C6)
Come here for crime fiction as well as science fiction and romance.
✉ **71-73 Charing Cross Rd WC2** ☎ **7734 3485** ⊖ **Tottenham Court Road** 🕐 Mon-Wed 10am-7pm, Thurs-Sat 10am-8pm

**Silver Moon** (6, C6)
Silver Moon has a shop within Folye's and specialises in books for, by and about women
✉ **113-119 Charing Cross Rd WC2** ☎ **7437 5660** **e** www.silver-moonbookshop.co.uk
⊖ **Tottenham Court Road** 🕐 Mon-Sat 9.30am-7.30pm & Sun 12-6pm

**Sportspages** (6, B6)
Magazines, fanzines and books about sport are the offerings here.
✉ **94-96 Charing Cross Rd WC2** ☎ **7240 9604**
**e** www.sportspages.co.uk ⊖ **Leicester Square, Tottenham Court Road**
🕐 Mon-Sat 9.30am-7pm, Sun 12-6pm

**Stanfords** (6, C6)
Stanfords has one of the world's largest and best selections of maps, guides and travel literature.
✉ **12-14 Long Acre WC2** ☎ **7836 1321**
**e** www.stanfords.co.uk ⊖ **Covent Garden**
🕐 Mon & Wed-Fri 9am-7.30pm, Tues 9.30am-7.30pm, Sat 10am-7pm, Sun 12-6pm

**The Travel Bookshop**
(2, E2) London's best 'boutique' travel bookshop has all the new guides as

## London Tales and True

Ever since Chaucer's pilgrims in *The Canterbury Tales* gathered for their trip at the Tabard Inn in Southwark, London has provided inspiration, or at least the backdrop, for writers, with Charles Dickens showing the capital at its best and very worst. In recent years Doris Lessing's collection of short stories *London Observed* contains some of the funniest and most vicious portrayals of the capital. *London Fields* by Martin Amis is heavy going; read his more acclaimed *Money*, set in Notting Hill, instead.

Other modern writers look at London from the perspective of its ethnic minorities: Hanif Kureishi about London's young Pakistanis in *The Black Album*; Caryl Phillips about Caribbean immigrants' experience in *The Final Passage*; and Zadie Smith about an English family and an immigrant Muslim one in north London in *White Teeth*. *Waterstone's Guide to London Writing* (£3.99), available at Waterstone's bookshops, has more listings.

well as out-of-print and antiquarian gems.

✉ **13 Blenheim Crescent W11** ☎ **7229 5260** **e** www.the travelbookshop.co.uk ⊖ **Ladbroke Grove** ☺ **Mon-Sat 10am-6pm, Sun 11am-4pm**

**Zwemmer Art & Architecture (6, B6)**
This shop stocks all kinds of art and architecture books. The branch (6, B6) opposite at 80 Charing Cross Rd specialises in books on photography and the cinema.

✉ **24 Litchfield St WC2** ☎ **7240 4158** **e** www.zwemmer.com ⊖ **Tottenham Court Road** ☺ **Mon-Wed & Fri 10am-6.30pm, Thurs 10am-8pm, Sat 10am-6pm**

*High-class Zwemmer*

# FOR CHILDREN

With that old dictum 'a child should be seen and not heard' a belief (though hardly a practice) in the UK, there's lots of shops selling toys, board games and books to keep the little terrors busy and, well, quieter.

**Benjamin Pollock's Toy Shop (6, C7)**
Pollock's is light years from the all-inclusive Hamleys. It's a quiet, charming, cluttered little shop that specialises in handmade toys.

✉ **44 The Market, Covent Garden WC2** ☎ **7379 7866** **e** www .pollocks-covent garden.co.uk ⊖ **Covent Garden** ☺ **Mon-Sat 10.30am-6pm, Sun 12-5pm**

## Shopping Guide

Shoppers who can't get enough should buy the annual *Time Out Shopping Guide* (£7.99), with details of virtually every shopping opportunity in the capital.

**Children's Book Centre (2, H3)**
This is a wonderful shop for children with standard books as well as the talking variety, videos, CDs and toys. Chocolates and jewellery are on offer too.

✉ **237 Kensington High St W8** ☎ **7937 7497** **e** www .childrensbookcentre.co .uk ⊖ **High Street Kensington** ☺ **Mon & Wed & Fri-Sat 9.30am-6.30pm, Tues 9.30am-6pm, Thurs 9.30am-7pm, Sun 12-6pm**

**Compendia (5, C2)**
This shop is piled high with board and other games, including a good selection of travel-themed ones.

✉ **10 The Market, Greenwich SE10** ☎ **8293 6616** 🚈 **DLR Cutty Sark** ☺ **Mon-Fri 12-5.30pm, Sat-Sun 10.30am-5.30pm**

**Daisy & Tom (3, J1)**
Gorgeous (and pricey) kids' clothes, shoes and toys are available here, with a marionette show, carousel rides and even haircuts (£6-12) to keep the kids occupied.

✉ **181-183 King's Rd SW3** ☎ **7352 5000** ⊖ **Sloane Square** ☺ **Mon-Tues & Thurs-Fri 10am-6pm, Wed 10am-7pm, Sat 10am-6.30pm, Sun 12-6pm**

**Hamleys (6, C3)**
This is an Aladdin's cave of toys and games, and the place to see every imaginable toy in the universe. The Lego Café on the top floor is a great place for kids to tarry.

✉ **188-196 Regent St W1** ☎ **7494 2000** **e** www.hamleys.com ⊖ **Oxford Circus** ☺ **Mon-Fri 10am-8pm, Sat 9.30am-8pm, Sun 12-6pm**

**Kite Store (6, B7)**
This shop stocks at least 100 different models as well as frisbees, boomerangs and other things that go whirr in the sky.

✉ **48 Neal St WC2** ☎ **7836 1666** ⊖ **Covent Garden** ☺ **Mon-Fri 10am-6pm, Sat 10.30am-6pm**

# places to eat

The growth in the number of restaurants and cafes – some 8500 at last count, representing 70 different cuisines – has made the city much more international. No matter what you fancy eating, there's bound to be a restaurant serving it. Things have improved remarkably since the 1970s – and why not? There was only one way but up from workers' 'caffs' serving greasy fried breakfasts and fish and chips deep-fried in rancid-smelling oil.

Just don't assume you'll get value for money here. We can't remember the number of times we've dined on over-refined Italian food or insipid (and ubiquitous) 'Modern European' accompanied by a single bottle of wine, dropped £35 or a £40 per head and wondered why we'd bothered. For that kind of money, this would be almost inconceivable in cities such as New York, Paris or Sydney. On the other hand we've had Pakistani food in Whitechapel, Turkish in Dalston and Vietnamese in Hackney that has made our hearts sing, our taste buds zing and our wallets only slightly lighter.

Eating out in London can be a real hit-and-miss affair. What we've done in this chapter is separate the wheat from the chaff. The restaurants, pubs and cafes listed here range from pretty good (convenient location, cheap price, unusual cuisine) to 'fantabulous' (worth a big splurge or journey). Hopefully this list will lead you in the right direction and you won't walk out wondering why *you* had bothered. *Bon appétit!*

### The Cost of a Meal

The pricing symbols we've used represent per person for dinner and generally include two courses and a drink. Count on paying up to 50% less for lunch.

| | |
|---|---|
| £ | Under £10 |
| ££ | £10-20 |
| £££ | £20-35 |
| ££££ | Over £35 |

### Booking Tables

Be aware that flavour-of-the-month restaurants in London can be booked up weeks – even months – in advance. Some places may ask for a credit-card number to confirm a booking. If you don't show up, a cancellation fee may be charged to your card; at least two places we know of charge £25 per person for no-shows. As a general rule, it's a good idea to make a reservation for the more expensive places (and even the less costly ones at weekends).

*Sit back and relax over a leisurely meal at your chosen destination.*

# BLOOMSBURY & CLERKENWELL

### Abeno (3, D7) ££
*Japanese*

This understated little Japanese restaurant specialises in *okonomiyaki*, a kind of Japanese omelette that is combined with the ingredients of your choice and cooked at the table.

✉ **47 Museum St WC1**
☎ **7405 3211**
⊖ **Tottenham Court Road** ⏰ **12-10pm** ♿

### Knosherie (3, D10) £
*Jewish*

Not kosher but kosher-style, this cafe-restaurant owned by the former director of Bloom's in Whitechapel has all the favourites: salt beef, cholent and rollmops.

✉ **12-13 Greville St**
☎ **7242 5190**
⊖ **Farringdon** ⏰ **24hrs**

### Le Café du Marché (3, C11) £££
*French*

Tucked away in a tiny alleyway near Smithfield Market, this rustic and very romantic place serves gutsy French fare and has live jazz on the 1st floor.

✉ **22 Charterhouse Sq, Charterhouse Mews EC1** ☎ **7608 1609**
⊖ **Farringdon** ⏰ **Mon-Fri 12-2.30pm & 6-10pm, Sat 6-10pm**

### Maison Novelli (3, C10) ££££
*French*

This is the sole survivor of the restaurant empire of chef Jean-Christophe Novelli. It continues to serve excellent (if pricey) Modern French food in a serene upstairs restaurant looking on to Clerkenwell Green.

✉ **29-31 Clerkenwell Green EC1** ☎ **7251 6606** ⊖ **Farringdon** ⏰ **Mon-Fri 12-3pm & 6-11pm, Sat 6-11pm** ♿ **V**

### Moro (3, B9) £££
*Moorish*

As its name implies, this place serves 'Moorish' cuisine, a tasty fusion of Spanish, Portuguese and North African flavours. It's a buzzy place with an open kitchen.

✉ **34-36 Exmouth Market N1** ☎ **7833 8336** ⊖ **Farringdon** ⏰ **Mon-Fri 12.30-2.30pm & 7-10.30pm, Sat 7-10.30pm** ♿

### North Sea Fish Restaurant (3, B7) ££
*British/Seafood*

The North Sea sets out to cook fresh fish and potatoes, a somewhat limited ambition in which it succeeds admirably: cod, haddock and plaice, deep-fried or grilled, served with a huge helping of chips.

✉ **7-8 Leigh St WC1**
☎ **7387 5892**
⊖ **Russell Square**
⏰ **12-2.30pm, Mon-Sat 5.30-10.30pm** ♿

### Rudland & Stubbs (3, D10) £££
*Seafood*

This 'oyster bar & dining room' serves up the freshest of the bivalves and local fish such as Cornish hake. It's jammed at lunch with City folk but quietens down at night.

✉ **35-37 Greenhill Rents, off Cowcross St EC1** ☎ **7253 0148**
⊖ **Farringdon**
⏰ **Mon-Fri 12-2.45pm & 6-10.45pm, Sat 7-10.45pm** ♿

### St John (3, C11) £££
*British*

This unadorned former warehouse is the place to come if you fancy sampling old-fashioned British dishes in new guises, such as whelks with pickled shallots and duck leg with carrots. This place is all about meat; after all, it is right next to Smithfield Market.

✉ **26 St John St EC1**
☎ **7251 0848**
⊖ **Farringdon** ⏰ **Mon-Fri 12-3pm, Mon-Sat 6-11pm** ♿

*A source of fresh veg up for grabs at a London market*

Simon Bracken

# BRIXTON & STOCKWELL

## Cuisine à la Brit

The most English of dishes is fish and chips: cod, plaice or haddock dipped in batter, deep-fried and served with chips (French fries) doused in vinegar and sprinkled with salt. But from the middle of the 19th century until just after WWII, the staple lunch for many Londoners was a pie filled with spiced eel and served with mashed potatoes and liquor (a parsley sauce). Nowadays the pies are usually meat-filled and the eel served smoked or jellied as a side dish. The best places to try these are **Manze's** near Bermondsey Market (see p. 78), **Goddards** in Greenwich (see p. 75) or **Porters** in Covent Garden (see p. 80).

### Bah Humbug
(2, K9)           ££
*Vegetarian*
Located in the disused crypt of a Methodist church, Bah Humbug is one of the best vegetarian restaurants in London with quite a global range – from Thai vegetable fritters to Cantonese mock duck and masala curry.
✉ St Matthew's Church, Brixton Hill SW2 ☎ 7738 3184 ⊖ Brixton ⏰ Mon-Thurs 5-11pm, Fri-Sat 5-11.30pm, Sun 1-5pm ♿ V

### Brixtonian Havana Club (2, K9)       £££
*Caribbean*
When in Rome... This Caribbean-inspired eatery blends West Indian, French, British and African influences to produce dishes such as roast pepper & ginger soup.
✉ 11 Beehive Pl SW9 ☎ 7924 9262 ⊖ Brixton ⏰ 12-3pm, Mon-Tues & Sun 7-10.30pm, Fri-Sat 7-11pm

### Café Portugal
(2, J9)           ££
*Portuguese*
Arguably the classiest option in Little Portugal (ie, the Stockwell neighbourhood), Café Portugal serves such Lusitanian favourites as *porco à Alentejana*, a tasty casserole of pork and clams, and *arroz de marisco* (seafood rice).
✉ 5a-6a Victoria House, South Lambeth Rd SW8 ☎ 7587 1962 ⊖ Brixton ⏰ 12-11pm ♿

### Satay Bar (2, K9)    ££
*Indonesian*
A favourite Asian eatery with Brixton trendies, the Satay Bar serves surprisingly authentic Indonesian food. Even more authentic are all the doors that open on to the busy street – you could easily be in a *warung* in Yogyakarta.
✉ 447-450 Coldharbour La SW9 ☎ 7326 5001 ⊖ Brixton ⏰ Mon-Fri 12-3pm & 6pm-midnight, Sat 1pm-midnight, Sun 1-10.30pm ♿

# CAMDEN & HAMPSTEAD

### Al Casbah (2, A5)    ££
*Middle Eastern*
Al Casbah is a small, friendly Moroccan restaurant with very good couscous and tajines.
✉ 45 Hampstead High St NW3 ☎ 7435 7632 ⊖ Hampstead ⏰ 5.30-11.30pm ♿ V

### Asakusa (4, E5)    ££
*Japanese*
For affordable Japanese, head to Asakusa for set menus such as prawn tempura with miso soup and rice.
✉ 265 Eversholt St NW1 ☎ 7388 8533 ⊖ Mornington Crescent ⏰ Mon-Fri 6-11.30pm, Sat 6-11pm ♿ V

### La Gaffe (2, A5)    £££
*Italian*
This comfortable, family-run restaurant, in an 18th-century cottage that is now a hotel, has been going forever.
✉ 107-111 Heath St NW3 ☎ 7794 7526 ⊖ Hampstead ⏰ Wed-Sun 12-2.30pm, Mon-Sun 6.30-11pm ♿

### Giraffe (2, A5)    ££
*International*
This colourful, upbeat place, with CDs for sale as well, is the culinary equivalent of world music, with everything from sashimi

salads and smoked salmon omelettes to Moroccan tea.
✉ **46 Rosslyn Hill NW3** ☎ 7435 0343 ⊖ Hamp-stead ⊘ Mon-Fri 8am-4pm & 5-11pm, Sat-Sun 12-5pm & 6-11pm ♿

**Lemonia** (4, C1) £££
*Greek*
This upmarket and very popular Greek restaurant offers good-value food and has a lively atmosphere.
✉ **89 Regent's Park Rd NW1** ☎ 7586 7454 ⊖ Chalk Farm ⊘ Mon-Fri & Sun 12-3pm, Mon-Sat 6-11pm ♿

**Mango Room**
(4, D4) ££
*West Indian*
This is an upmarket, refined choice for island food, with

delightful starters such as fluffy crab and potato balls and unusual mains such as a platter of cooked vegetables including ackee, a yellow-skinned Jamaican fruit.
✉ **10 Kentish Town Rd NW1** ☎ 7482 5065 ⊖ Camden Town ⊘ Tues-Sun 12-3pm, Mon-Sun 6pm-midnight ♿ **V**

**Trojka** (4, C1) ££
*Eastern European/Russian*
Trojka serves good-value Eastern European/Russian dishes such as herrings with dill sauce and Polish *bigosz* (a cabbage 'stew' with mixed meats) in an attractive, sky-lit restaurant. It has a house wine but it is also BYO (corkage

fee charged).
✉ **101 Regents Park Rd NW1** ☎ 7483 3765 ⊖ Chalk Farm ⊘ 12-10.30pm ♿

*Kitted out in a stripy pinny*

# CHELSEA, SOUTH KENSINGTON, EARL'S COURT & PIMLICO

**Bibendum**
(2, H5) ££££
*Modern British*
This Conran establishment is in one of London's finest settings for a restaurant, the Art Nouveau Michelin House (1911). The popular

**Bibendum Oyster Bar** is on the ground floor, where you really feel at the heart of the architectural finery. Upstairs it's all much lighter and brighter.
✉ **81 Fulham Rd SW3** ☎ 7581 5817 ⊖ South Kensington ⊘ Mon-Fri 12-2.30pm & 7-11.30pm, Sat 12.30-3pm & 7-11.30pm, Sun 12.30-3pm & 7-10.30pm ♿

**Daquise** (2, H5) ££
*Polish*
Daquise is a real dinosaur – a loveable little Tyrannosaurus rex indeed – and close to the museums. It's a rather shabby-looking Polish cafe/diner, with a good range of vodkas and

extremely reasonably priced food.
✉ **20 Thurloe St SW7** ☎ 7589 6117 ⊖ South Kensington ⊘ 11.30am-11pm ♿

**Krungtap** (2, J4) ££
*Thai*
Krungtap (the Thai name for Bangkok) is a busy, friendly cafe with karaoke from 7pm to midnight Friday to Sunday.
✉ **227 Old Brompton Rd SW10** ☎ 7259 2314 ⊖ Sloane Square ⊘ 12-4pm & 6-11pm ♿ **V**

**La Poule au Pot**
(2, H7) £££
*French*
Some Londoners claim the 'Chicken in the Pot' is the

### Tipping
Many London restaurants include a 'discretionary' service charge (average around 12.5%), which should be clearly indicated on the bill. At places that don't levy a charge you are expected to leave a 10-15% tip unless the service was unsatisfactory.

best country-style French restaurant in town. The alfresco front terrace is a lovely spot in the warmer months.
✉ **231 Ebury St SW1**
☎ **7730 7763**
⊖ **Sloane Square**
⏲ Mon-Sat 12.30-2.30pm & 7-11.15pm, Sun 12.30-2.30pm & 7-10.30pm ♿

**Roussillon** (2, J7) **££££**
*French*
This is one of the best independently owned French restaurants in London and

service is as seamless as everything that emerges from the kitchen. Encore!
✉ **16 St Barnabas St SW1** ☎ **7730 5550**
⊖ **Sloane Square**
⏲ Mon-Fri 12-2.30pm & 6.30-10.30pm, Sat 6.30-10.30pm

Simon Bracken

## Business Munch

Some good places to mix business and the pleasure of dining include:

**Maison Novelli** (p. 70)
**St John** (p. 70)
**Moro** (p. 70)
**Café Spice Namaste** (below)
**Blue Print Café** (p. 77)
**Oxo Tower** (p. 78)
**Les Trois Garçons** (below)

# EAST END & THE CITY

**Arkansas Café**
(3, C15) **££**
*American*
This no-frills barbecue run by American Bubba Helberg produces some of the finest American-style grills in London: steaks, chicken, sausage, ribs.
✉ **Unit 12, Spitalfields Market, 107b Commercial St E1**
☎ **7377 6999**
⊖ **Liverpool Street, Aldgate East** ⏲ Mon-Fri 12-2.30pm, Sun 12-4pm ♿

**Café Spice Namaste**
(2, F13) **£££**
*Indian*
One of our favourite Indian restaurants in London, Namaste serves Goan and Keralan cuisine (with South-East Asian hints) in an old courthouse that has been decorated in 'carnival' colours.
✉ **16 Prescot St E1**
☎ **7488 9242** ⊖ **Tower Hill** ⏲ Mon-Fri 12-3pm & 6.15-10.30pm, Sat 6.30-10.30pm ♿ **V**

**Les Trois Garçons**
(3, B15) **££££**
*French*
Walk through the door of this enormous erstwhile pub and your jaw will drop open: giraffe heads stick out from the wall at right angles, stuffed swans wear tiaras and the mirrors are listed. The food – classic French – is good if not excellent and at least one of the eponymous 'three boys' is always on hand to meet and greet.
✉ **1 Club Row E1**
☎ **7613 1924** ⊖ **Old Street, Liverpool Street** ⏲ Mon-Thurs 12-2.30pm & 7-10pm, Fri-Sat 12-2.30pm & 7-10.30pm

**Mesón Los Barriles**
(3, C15) **££**
*Spanish/Tapas*
This place in Spitalfields Market has an excellent selection of tapas, and fish and seafood main courses.
✉ **8a Lamb St E1**
☎ **7375 3136**
⊖ **Liverpool Street**
⏲ Mon-Fri 11am-11pm, Sun 12-4pm ♿

**New Tayyab**
(2, E13) **£**
*Indian/Pakistani*
This restaurant has some of the most authentic Indian and Pakistani food this side of Delhi and Karachi. Choose your *seekh* kebabs, lamb chops or one of several *karahi* (a small wok) dishes, then select a vegetable of your choice and one of several *dahls*. It's BYO only.
✉ **83 Fieldgate St E1**
☎ **7247 9543**
⊖ **Whitechapel**
⏲ 5pm-midnight ♿

**The Quiet Revolution**
(3, B11) **££**
*Vegetarian*
The food at this large and bright cafe is not 100% vegetarian (there are a couple of meat and fish dishes lurking about) but it is all organic.
✉ **49 Old St EC1**
☎ **7253 5556**
⊖ **Old Street**
⏲ Mon-Fri 9am-10pm, Sat-Sun 10am-4pm ♿

**The Real Greek**
(3, B14) **£££**
*Greek*
This place serves what could almost be called Modern Greek food – eg, hotpot of kid with dandelion and leek fricassée – to an appreciative boho crowd.
✉ 15 Hoxton Market N1 ☎ 7739 8212
⊖ Old Street
⏱ 12-3pm, Mon-Sat 5.30-10.30pm ♿

**Ye Olde Cheshire Cheese** (3, E10) **£££**
*British*
Rebuilt shortly after the Great Fire of 1666 and popular with Dr Johnson, Thackeray, Dickens and the visiting Mark Twain, the Cheshire Cheese is touristy but the traditional Chop Room is a good place to take visitors.
✉ Wine Office Court, off Fleet St EC4
☎ 7353 6170
⊖ Blackfriars ⏱ Mon-Sat 12-9pm, Sun 12-2.30pm ♿

**Whitechapel Art Gallery Café** (3, D15) **£**
*Vegetarian*
This vegetarian place is upstairs from the gallery and serves dishes such as spinach Florentine, salad and soups.
✉ 80-82 Whitechapel High St E1 ☎ 7522 7888 ⊖ Aldgate East
⏱ Tues & Thurs-Sun 1am-5pm, Wed 1am-8pm ♿ **V**

*Best of ye olde British*

# FULHAM & HAMMERSMITH

**The Gate** (2, J1) **££**
*Vegetarian*
This restaurant, with its beautifully presented, unusual (and meatless) main courses, may be the place to convert your carnivorous counterparts to the world of vegetarianism.
✉ 51 Queen Caroline St W6 ☎ 8748 6932
⊖ Hammersmith
⏱ Mon-Fri 12-3pm, Mon-Sat 6-10.45pm ♿ **V**

**River Café**
(2, J1) **££££**
*Italian*
The very buzzy, see-and-scene River Café owes its fame as much to the cookbooks it has spawned as to the food actually served here, but it does have very good Modern Italian cuisine.
✉ Thames Wharf, Rainville Rd W6
☎ 7381 8824 ⊖ Hammersmith ⏱ 12.30-3pm, Mon-Sat 7-9.30pm ♿

**Vama** (2, J5) **£££**
*Indian*
Vama serves unusual dishes from the North-West Frontier and other regions of India in a lovely dining room. There's also a decent Sunday buffet with jazz.
✉ 438 King's Rd SW10
☎ 7351 4118
⊖ Fulham Broadway
🚌 11, 22
⏱ 12.30pm-3pm & 6.30-11.30pm
♿ **V**

### Self-Servings
The best way to keep eating prices down is to self-cater. Look for a **Tesco** or smaller **Tesco Metro** branch, with outlets at: Covent Garden, 21 Bedford St WC2 (6, C7); opposite Liverpool Street Station, 156 Bishopsgate EC2 (3, D14); the City, 80b Cheapside EC2 (3, E12); 311 Oxford St W1 (3, E3); Notting Hill, 224 Portobello Rd W11 (2, E2); and Canary Wharf, Canada Square E14 (1, B5). Branches of **Safeway**, **Asda** and **Sainsbury's**, found throughout the city, are also competitively priced. **Waitrose** is more upmarket and expensive.

*Spoilt for cheesy choices at a London deli counter*

# GREENWICH

## Veggie Victuals

Vegetarianism is very much an accepted part of the restaurant scene, and it's rare to find somewhere that does not offer at least a couple of dishes for those who don't eat meat.

Two of the best vegetarian restaurants in London are **Carnevale** (135 Whitecross St EC1; 3, C12; ☎ 7250 3452; **e** www.carnevalerestaurant.co.uk; ⊖ Barbican) and **Country Life** (3-4 Warwick St; 6, 3C; ☎ 7434 2922; **e** www.countryliferestaurant.co.uk'; ⊖ Piccadilly Circus).

### Goddards Pie House
(5, C2)                £
*British*
Goddards is truly a step back in time: a real London caff with wooden benches and things such as steak and kidney pie with liquor and mash and shepherd's pie with beans and a rich brown gravy. There are also fruit-based sweet pies.
✉ 45 Greenwich Church St SE10 ☎ 8293 9313 🚆 DLR Cutty Sark ⌚ Tues-Fri & Sun 1am-3pm, Sat 10.45am-4.30pm ♿

### North Pole
(5, E1)              £££
*International*
This pleasant place has a bar/pub on the ground floor and an excellent, if somewhat stuffy (chintz drapes etc), restaurant on the 1st floor. There's a popular Sunday breakfast (9.30am-noon) and brunch (12-6.30pm) and a 10-15% discount on dinner Monday to Thursday.
✉ 131 Greenwich High Rd SE10 ☎ 8853 3020 🚆 DLR Greenwich ⌚ Mon-Sat 12-3pm & 7-10.30pm, Sun 12-3pm & 7-10pm

### Time (5, C2)        £££
*International*
This bar, gallery and restaurant is many things to many people and dishes up Modern European in what used to be a 19th-century music hall.
✉ 7a College Approach SE10 ☎ 8305 9767 🚆 DLR Cutty Sark ⌚ Mon-Sat 12-11.30pm, Sun 12-10.30pm **V**

# ISLINGTON & STOKE NEWINGTON

### Angel Mangal
(2, C10)               ££
*Turkish*
Angel Mangal serves some of the best Turkish meze, grilled lamb chops and pigeon cooked over a smoking *ocakbasi* (wood-fired brazier) and salads in north London.
✉ 139 Upper St N1 ☎ 7359 7777 ⊖ Highbury & Islington, Angel ⌚ noon-midnight ♿ **V**

### Primos Lounge
(2, B10)              £££
*Italian*
This gem of a place serves some of the best Italian food in London (not just the standard pasta and pizza but superb mains too). The decor is modern and upbeat, the front bar always lively and the service warm and efficient.
✉ 54 Islington Park St N1 ☎ 7354 5717 ⊖ Highbury & Islington, Angel ⌚ noon-midnight ♿

### Rasa (2, A12)        ££
*Vegetarian*
This no-smoking South Indian vegetarian restaurant gets rave reviews (and attracts queues) for dishes not often seen (or tasted) outside private homes.
✉ 55 Stoke Newington Church St N16 ☎ 7249 0344 🚆 Stoke Newington 🚌 73 ⌚ Mon-Thurs 6-11pm, Fri 6pm-midnight, Sat-Sun 12-3pm & 6pm-midnight ♿ **V**

### Ravi Shankar
(3, A10)                £
*Vegetarian*
This small, inexpensive restaurant has some of the best Indian vegetarian food in London.
✉ 422 St John St EC1 ☎ 7833 5849 ⊖ Angel ⌚ 12-10.30pm ♿ **V**

### Tartuf (2, C10)       £
*French (Alsatian)*
This place serves *tartes flambées* (or *flammekuchen* in Alsatian), a filling dish that is a thin layer of pastry topped with cream, onion, bacon and sometimes cheese or mushrooms and cooked in a wood-fired oven.
✉ 88 Upper St N1 ☎ 7288 0954 ⊖ Angel

🕐 **Mon-Fri 12-2.30pm & 5-11.30pm, Sat-Sun 12-2.30pm** ♿

**Yellow River Café**
**(2, B10)** ££
*Asian*
This is part of an upbeat chain serving eclectic Asian cuisine under the watchful gaze (note the Warhol-style series of portraits) of American TV chef Ken Hom.
✉ **206 Upper St N1**
☎ **7354 8833** ⊖ **Highbury & Islington, Angel** 🕐 **Mon-Wed 12-3pm & 5.30-11pm, Thurs-Sat 12-3pm & 5.30-11.30pm** ♿ **V**

*Oodles of noodles*

# KENSINGTON & KNIGHTSBRIDGE

**Fifth Floor (3, H1) £££**
*International*
This restaurant, bar and cafe at Harvey Nichols department store is the perfect place to drop after you've shopped. It's quite expensive, but there's a good value two- and three-course set lunch.
✉ **Harvey Nichols, 109-125 Knightsbridge SW1** ☎ **7823 1839** ⊖ **Knightsbridge**
🕐 **Mon-Fri 12-3pm & 6-11pm, Sat 12-3.30pm** & 6-11pm, Sun 12-3.30pm ♿ **V**

**Ognisko Polskie**
**(2, G5)** £££
*Polish*
The 'Polish Hearth' is the Poland of another world and time, with reasonably priced food served in a clubby dining room filled with portraits, chandeliers and mirrors.
✉ **55 Prince's Gate SW7**
☎ **7589 4635** ⊖ **South Kensington** 🕐 **12-11pm**

**Parisienne Chophouse**
**(2, H6)** £££
*French*
Marco Pierre White is again trying to change the face of Londoners' eating habits. This time he sets out to create unpretentious, un-fused (and -fussed) French food and succeeds marvellously.
✉ **3 Yeoman's Row SW3**
☎ **7590 9999** ⊖ **South Kensington** 🕐 **Mon-Sat 12-3pm & 5.30-11pm, Sun 12-3.30pm & 6pm-10pm** ♿

# NOTTING HILL, BAYSWATER & PADDINGTON

**Café Grove (2, E2)** £
*Cafe*
Head here for gigantic and imaginative breakfasts (chilli sausages, pints of cappuccino) as well as cheap and cheerful vegetarian. The large balcony overlooking the market is great for watching all the action on a weekend morning.
✉ **253a Portobello Rd**
☎ **7243 1094** ⊖ **Ladbroke Grove** 🕐 **Mon-Fri 9.3am-5.30pm, Sat 9.30am-6pm, Sun 10.30am-5pm** ♿ **V**

**Geales (2, F3)** ££
*Seafood*
This popular fish restaurant, established in 1939, prices everything according to weight and season. It regularly gets the vote for the best fish and chips in London.
✉ **2 Farmer St W8**
☎ **7727 7528**
⊖ **Notting Hill Gate**
🕐 **Mon-Sat 12-3pm & 6-11pm, Sun 6-10.30pm** ♿

**L'Accento (2, F4)** £££
*Italian*
This simply decorated restaurant offers a two-course set menu, which could include mussel stew in white wine, followed by roast leg of lamb with balsamic vinegar. Once you step away from this menu, L'Accento becomes a lot more expensive. It's a good idea to book ahead.
✉ **16 Garway Rd W2**
☎ **7243 2201** ⊖ **Bayswater** 🕐 **Mon-Sat 12-2.30pm & 6.30-11.15pm, Sun 6.30-11.15pm** ♿

**Mandola (2, F3)** ££
*African*
Mandola offers something different: vegetarian Sudanese dishes such as *tamia*, a kind of felafel, and *fifilia*, a vegetable curry. Meat dishes include chicken *halla* and *shorba fule*, an unusual meat and peanut soup.
✉ **139-141 Westbourne Grove W2**
☎ **7229 4734** ⊖ **Bayswater** 🕐 **Mon-Sat 12-11.30pm, Sun 12-10.30pm** ♿ **V**

**Satay House** (2, E5) ££
*Malaysian*
A trip to Paddington does not have to mean just catching the Heathrow Express. This place serves some of the most authentic Malaysian food in north London.
✉ 13 Sale Pl W2

☎ 7723 6763
⊖ Bayswater ⏰ 12-3pm, 6-11pm ♿

**Veronica's** (2, F3)  £££
*British*
Veronica's is trying to establish the idea that England does have a

culinary heritage, with some fascinating dishes going back as early as the 14th century.
✉ 3 Hereford Rd W2
☎ 7229 5079
⊖ Bayswater ⏰ Mon-Fri 12-2.30pm & 6-11.30pm, Sat 6-11.30pm

## SOUTH OF THE THAMES

**Blue Print Café**
(3, H15)               £££
*International*
Modern European cooking is the order of the day at this flagship Conran restaurant. There are spectacular views of the river from here.
✉ Design Museum, Butlers Wharf SE1
☎ 7378 7031
⊖ Tower Hill ⏰ Mon-Sat 12-3pm & 6-11pm, Sun 12-3pm ♿ Ⓥ

**fish!** (3, G13)        £££
*Seafood*
In a glassed-in Victorian pavilion overlooking Borough Market and Southwark Cathedral, fish! serves fresher-than-fresh fish and seafood prepared simply and served with one of five sauces.
✉ Cathedral St SE1
☎ 7234 3333 ⊖ London Bridge ⏰ Mon-Sat 11.30am-10.30pm, Sun 12-10pm ♿

**Honest Cabbage**
(2, G12)                 ££
*Modern British*
This well-received bohemian restaurant with an ever-changing blackboard menu offers everything from soups, salads, sandwiches and pies to mains such as monkfish with star anise and sweet chilli.
✉ 99 Bermondsey St

SE1 ☎ 7234 0080
⊖ London Bridge
⏰ Mon-Wed 12-3pm & 6.30-10pm, Thurs-Fri 12-3pm & 6.30-11pm, Sat 7-11pm Ⓥ

**Konditor & Cook**
(3, H10)                  £
*Cafe*
This cafe at the Young Vic serves meals through-

out the day; however, we come here for the pastries and cake made by arguably the best 'bespoke' bakery in London.
✉ 66 The Cut SE1
☎ 7620 2700
⊖ Waterloo ⏰ Mon-Fri 8.30am-11pm, Sat 10.30am-11pm ♿ Ⓥ

### Dining Rooms with a View

For great views from the comfort of a restaurant you couldn't do much better than the 8th floor of the **Oxo Tower** (p. 78) or even **People's Palace** (p. 78) on the 3rd floor of the Royal Festival Hall. A more down-to-earth approach is looking at the city and its bridges from one of the riverside pubs such as the **Anchor** (p. 93). Some people like the views across Hyde Park from the **Windows on the World** bar on the 28th floor of the Hilton Hotel, Park La W1 (3, H2; ⊖ Hyde Park Corner). Those on a budget should grab some fish & chips and head for Waterloo Bridge at sunset. There's no finer view of London.

Simon Bracken

*Eight floors up in the Oxo Tower*

## Manze's (2, H12) £
*British*
London's oldest pie shop is still going strong after a century of trading. Handy to the Bermondsey Market, Manze's serves masses of jellied eels, and pie, mash and liquor in a pleasantly tiled interior.

✉ 87 Tower Bridge Rd SE1 ☎ 7407 2985
⊖ London Bridge
🕐 Mon 1am-2pm, Tues-Thurs 10.30am-2pm, Fri 1am-2.15pm, Sat 1am-2.45pm ♿

## Oxo Tower
(3, F10) ££££
*International*
The food here – a bit Mediterranean, a bit French, some Pacific Rim – is satisfactory in that Fifth Floor sort of way (it's owned by Harvey Nichols) but most people come here for the view. If you can't get in there's always the cheaper

Culinary heights?

## Kosher Restaurants
Searching for a kosher meal in central London is a joyless task, though for simple Ashkenazic favourites there's always **Reubens** at (79 Baker Street W1; 3, D1; ☎ 7486 0035 ⊖ Baker Street). Middle Eastern and Sephardic-style dishes can be had at **Solly's** (148a Golders Green Rd NW11; 1, B4; ☎ 8455 2121 ⊖ Golders Green). The London Beth Din Kashrut Division (☎ 8343 6255; e www.kosher.org.uk) is the place to contact for information on kosher eating in London.

*Ready and waiting*

Bistrot 2 Riverside (☎ 7498 8200) on the 2nd floor of the tower.
✉ 8th fl, Barge House St SE1 ☎ 7803 3888
⊖ Waterloo 🕐 Mon-Sat 12-3pm & 5.30-11.30pm, Sun 12-4pm & 5.30-10.30pm ♿ V

## People's Palace
(6, E9) £££
*International*
Easy to miss inside the Royal Festival Hall and boasting some fine views of the Thames and the City, this rather deceptively named restaurant is the perfect place to head before or after a South Bank performance.
✉ L3, Royal Festival Hall SE1 ☎ 7839 6669
⊖ Waterloo
🕐 12-3pm & 5.30-11pm ♿

## RSJ (3, G9) £££
*French*
This rather industrially named place (most Britons know RSJ as a 'rolled steel joist') nonetheless serves comforting classic French dishes.
✉ 13a Coin St SE1 ☎ 7928 4554
⊖ Waterloo
🕐 Mon-Fri 12-2pm & 5.30-11pm, Sat 5.30-11pm ♿

## Ransome's Dock
(2, K5) £££
*Modern British*
Diners flock to Ransome's Dock not because it is located on a narrow inlet of the Thames but to sample its superbly prepared Modern British food and its homely atmosphere.
✉ 35-37 Parkgate Rd SW11 ☎ 7223 1611
⊖ Sloane Square
🚌 19, 49, 239, 319 or 345 🕐 Mon-Fri 12-11pm, Sat noon-midnight, Sun 12-3.30pm ♿

# THE WEST END: SOHO TO THE STRAND

## Belgo Centraal
(6, B6)    ££
*Belgian*
Taking the lift down to the basement and walking through the kitchens is all part of the fun at Belgo, where the waiters dress up as 16th-century monks. This being a Belgian restaurant, mussels and chips/French fries are the specialities, and beer (100 different flavoured pilsners) is the drink.
✉ 50 Earlham St WC2
☎ 7813 2233
⊖ Covent Garden
⏰ Sun-Mon
12-10.30pm, Tues-Sat
12-11.30pm ♿

## Café in the Crypt
(6, D6)    £
*International*
Good food, with plenty of vegetarian offerings, can be had in this atmospheric crypt beneath St Martin-in-the-Fields church (though graveside dining is not for the squeamish). Lunchtimes in the crypt are often hectic and noisy.
✉ St Martin-in-the-Fields, Duncannon St WC2 ☎ 7839 4342
⊖ Charing Cross
⏰ 12- 3.15pm, Mon-Wed 5-7.30pm, Thurs-Sat 8.30-10.30pm ♿ V

## Chiang Mai (6, B5)  ££
*Thai*
A relatively pricey Thai restaurant, Chiang Mai has a separate vegetarian menu and a wide range of soups on offer.
✉ 48 Frith St W1
☎ 7437 7444
⊖ Tottenham Court Road ⏰ 12-4pm & 6-11pm ♿ V

## Criterion (6, D4)   £££
*Modern French*
This place on Piccadilly Circus has a spectacular interior that one breathless diner has compared to the inside of a Fabergé egg. The menu offers fashionable Modern French food, but there are also some English classics such as fish and chips.
✉ 224 Piccadilly W1
☎ 7930 0488 ⊖ Piccadilly Circus ⏰ Mon-Sat 12-2.30pm & 5.30-11.30pm, Sun 5.30-10.30pm ♿

## Gay Hussar
(6, A5)    £££
*Hungarian*
This is the Soho of the 1950s, when grandiose dining took place in rooms with brocade and sepia prints on the walls. And they serve enormous Hungarian portions!
✉ 2 Greek St W1
☎ 7437 0973
⊖ Tottenham Court Road ⏰ 12.15-2.30pm, Mon-Sat 5.30-10.45pm ♿

## Gerrard's Corner
(6, C5)    ££
*Chinese*
This is one of the more reliable Chinese restaurants in Chinatown, both for quality and good value.
✉ 30 Wardour St WC2
☎ 7437 0984
⊖ Leicester Square
⏰ Mon-Sat 12-11.30pm, Sun 1pm-10.15pm ♿ V

## Gopal's of Soho
(6, B5)    ££
*Indian*
Gopal's offers reasonably authentic food at affordable prices in a (at long last)

recently renovated restaurant. If you can't tell your curry from your chutney try a *thali*, a set meal served on circular metal trays.
✉ 12 Bateman St W1
☎ 7434 0840 ⊖ Tottenham Court Road
⏰ noon-midnight ♿ V

Simon Bracken

*The doors to gastro-heaven*

## The Ivy (6, B6)    £££
*Modern British*
With its liveried doorman and celebrity clientele, The Ivy is a showbizzy event in itself. The English menu includes dishes such as shepherd's pie, potted shrimps and kedgeree.
✉ 1 West St WC2
☎ 7836 4751
⊖ Leicester Square, Tottenham Court Road
⏰ Mon-Sat 12-3pm & 5.30pm-midnight, Sun 12-3.30pm & 5pm-midnight

## Jen (6, C5)    ££
*Chinese*
This primarily hotpot restaurant does scores of other Chinese dishes (both old favourites and more innovative dishes) and is

always packed with Chinese diners.

✉ 7 Gerrard St W1
☎ 7287 8193
⊖ Leicester Square
⏱ noon-3am 🌡 V

### Joe Allen (6, C8)　£££
*American*

A long-established American-style eatery, this is a star-spotter's paradise. There's a real buzz here and it can get crowded. Starters and main dishes (lamb chops, grilled halibut etc) are varied, with some good vegetarian options.

✉ 13 Exeter St WC2
☎ 7836 0651
⊖ Covent Garden
⏱ Mon-Fri noon-12.45am, Sat 11.30am-12.45am, Sun 11.30am-11.30pm 🌡

### Kettners (6, B5)　££
*Italian*

If you fancy something with fewer links than the Pizza Express chain, Kettners serves up similar fare but in a wonderful atmosphere of gently fading grandeur, with a piano tinkling in the background.

✉ 29 Romilly St W1

☎ 7734 6112
⊖ Leicester Square
⏱ noon-midnight 🌡

### Kulu Kulu (6, C4)　££
*Japanese*

This place is generally believed to serve up London's best conveyor-belt sushi.

✉ 76 Brewer St W1
☎ 7734 7316
⊖ Piccadilly Circus
⏱ Mon-Fri 12-2.30pm & 5-10pm, Sat 12-3.45pm & 5-10pm 🌡

### Maison Bertaux (6, B5)　£
*Cafe*

Bertaux has been turning out confections for 130 years, and they're still as exquisite as ever. There's a tearoom on the 1st floor.

✉ 28 Greek St W1
☎ 7437 6007 ⊖ Tottenham Court Road
⏱ 9am-8pm 🌡 V

### Mildred's (6, B5)　££
*Vegetarian*

Mildred's is so small (and popular) that you may have to share a table. It's worth it, though, because the vegetarian food is both good and well priced.

✉ 58 Greek St W1
☎ 7494 1634

### Eating Words

For hundreds of up-to-the minute reviews of London's eateries, check out Lonely Planet's *Out to Eat – London*, now in its second edition, which provides comprehensive coverage of the city's best restaurants, cafes and gastropubs.

⊖ Tottenham Court Road ⏱ Mon-Sat 12-11pm 🌡 V

### Momo (6, C3)　£££
*Middle Eastern*

The kasbah comes to London at this trendy and expensive Moroccan restaurant, with excellent couscous and tajines. **Mô Bazaar**, Momo's 'salad bar, tearoom and bazaar' next door, is a cheaper, more relaxed place.

✉ 25 Heddon St W1
☎ 7434 4040
⊖ Piccadilly Circus
⏱ 12-2.30pm, Mon-Sat 6-10pm 🌡 V

### Porters (6, C7)　££
*British*

Porters specialises in pies, long a staple of English cooking but not regularly found on modern menus. They have the usual ones such as steak and kidney pie and pudding and the less common – lamb and apricot or chicken and broccoli – as well as fish and chips.

✉ 17 Henrietta St WC2
☎ 7836 6466
⊖ Covent Garden
⏱ Mon-Sat 12-11.30pm, Sun 12-10.30pm 🌡

*To eat in or take out?*

Neil Setchfield

**Rainforest Café** (6, C4) ££
*American*
A Hard Rock Café for kids, with animatronic birds and beasts roaring and hooting in a 'jungle', Rainforest Café serves American food such as burgers with a splash of Tex-Mex and Caribbean.
**✉ 20 Shaftesbury Ave W1 ☎ 7434 3111 ⊖ Piccadilly Circus ⌚ Mon-Fri 12-10pm, Sat 12-8pm, Sun 11.30am-10pm 🚼 V**

**Rock & Sole Plaice** (6, A7) ££
*British*
This no-nonsense fish and chips shop has basic Formica tables and delicious cod or haddock in batter on the ground floor, and more elaborate seating downstairs.
**✉ 47 Endell St WC2 ☎ 7836 3785 ⊖ Covent Garden ⌚ Mon-Sat 11.30am-10pm, Sun 12-9pm 🚼**

**Soup Works** (6, B4) £
*International*
This place, which deals in (and serves up) the 'Alchemy of Soup', is a popular lunchtime venue.
**✉ 9 D'Arblay St W1 ☎ 7439 7687 ⊖ Oxford Circus ⌚ Mon-Sat 8am-5pm 🚼 V**

**Spiga** (6, B4) ££
*Italian*
This is where to head if you want authentic pizza, pasta or an Italian main dish in sleek, pleasant surroundings but don't want to pay the earth for it.
**✉ 84-86 Wardour St W1 ☎ 7734 3444 ⊖ Tottenham Court Road ⌚ Mon-Tues 12-3pm & 6-11pm, Wed-Sat 12-3pm & 6pm-midnight, Sun 1-4pm & 6-11pm 🚼**

**Sports Café** (6, E5) ££
*International*
There's no escaping sport at this restaurant, with a dance floor, pool tables, mini basketball court and arcade games. Some 140 table-side TVs and four big screens keep you occupied with the latest games while you await your burger and chips.
**✉ 80 Haymarket SW1 ☎ 7839 8300 ⊖ Piccadilly Circus ⌚ Mon-Thurs noon-2am, Fri-Sat noon-3am, Sun 12-10.30pm**

**Sugar Club** (6, C3) £££
*International*
This popular place concentrates on Pacific Rim dishes – grilled scallops with sweet chilli sauce, roast duck on wok-fried black beans – that cleverly mix and match traditions of east and west.
**✉ 21 Warwick St W1 ☎ 7437 7776 ⊖ Oxford Circus ⌚ Mon-Sat 12-3pm & 6-10.30pm, Sun 12.30-3pm & 6-10.30pm 🚼**

**Tokyo Diner** (6, C5) £
*Japanese*
The Tokyo Diner is a good-value place to stop for a quick bowl of noodles or plate of sushi before the cinema or theatre.
**✉ 2 Newport Pl WC2 ☎ 7287 8777 ⊖ Leicester Square ⌚ noon-midnight 🚼 V**

**Yo! Sushi** (6, B3) ££
*Japanese*
Yo! Sushi is one of London's livelier sushi bars, where diners sit around the bar and the dishes come to them via a 60m-long conveyor belt (drinks, on the other hand, are served by tiny robots). There are branches at Selfridges (p. 59; 3, E2; ☎ 7318 3944) and on the 5th Floor of Harvey Nichols (p. 58; 3, H1; ☎ 7201 8641).
**✉ 52 Poland St W1 ☎ 7287 0443 ⊖ Oxford Circus ⌚ Mon-Sat 12-11pm, Sun 12-11pm 🚼**

**Zilli Fish** (6, C4) £££
*Italian*
This place serves passable Italian-inspired seafood dishes, but it's more about the surrounds (buzzy) and your fellow diners (minor celebs and media hounds) than the food.
**✉ 36-40 Brewer St W1 ☎ 7734 8649 ⊖ Piccadilly Circus ⌚ Mon-Sat 12-11.30pm 🚼**

Simon Bracken

*Get some food under your belt at Yo! Sushi.*

# HIGH TEA

Given the important role that tea has always played in English culture, it should be no surprise that going out for 'afternoon tea' is something dear to the hearts of Londoners. In most circles these days, however, it's more of a special occasion than a daily routine.

A traditional set 'high tea' comes with a selection of delicate sandwiches (eg, cucumber and smoked salmon), scones with cream and jam, rich desserts and lots and lots of tea.

## Brown's Hotel
(6, D2)  £££

Brown's Hotel dispenses tea in the Drawing Room every day, with a pianist to soothe away any lingering stress from the bustling streets outside. It's advisable to book.

✉ 30 Albemarle St W1 ☎ 7493 6020
⊖ Green Park
◷ 3-6pm ⚹ V

## Claridge's (6, C1)  £££

Claridge's serves tea (and 'champagne tea') in its grand 18th-century foyer. The opulent surrounds, elegant staff and fine cakes make this one of the best teas in town so booking is essential and men must wear jacket and tie.

✉ Brook St W1
☎ 7629 8860
⊖ Bond Street
◷ 3-5.30pm
⚹ V

## Fortnum & Mason
(3, G4)  ££

This celebrated retailer serves afternoon tea at its 4th-floor St James restaurant. It's a slightly less expensive tea than at the hotels, and booking ahead is advised.

✉ 181 Piccadilly W1
☎ 7734 8040
⊖ Piccadilly Circus
◷ Mon-Sat 3-5.45pm
⚹ V

## Le Meridien Waldorf
(6, B8)  £££

High tea is served weekdays at the Waldorf in the splendidly restored Palm Court. At the weekend there's a chance to take part in the old-fashioned ritual of tea dancing, when booking is essential and prices rise.

✉ Aldwych WC2
☎ 7836 2400
⊖ Charing Cross
◷ Mon-Fri 3-5.30pm, Sat 2.30-5.30pm, Sun 4-6.30pm
⚹ V

*Fancy a scone or three?*

Neil Setchfield

## Orangery (2, G4)  £/££

This graceful park cafe in Kensington Gardens is a superb place to have a relatively affordable set tea; choose from one with cucumber sandwiches or scones or the more expensive champagne tea.

✉ Kensington Gardens W8 ☎ 7938 1406
⊖ Queensway
◷ Mar-Oct 1-6pm, Nov-Feb 1-5pm ⚹ V

## The Ritz (6, E2)  £££

The Ritz is probably the best-known place to take tea, although these days it's become something of a production-line process – the splendour of the florid pink and gold surroundings notwithstanding. You need to book a month ahead for weekdays and up to six weeks in advance for weekends for one of two seatings. Men must wear jacket and tie.

✉ 150 Piccadilly W1
☎ 7493 8181 ⊖ Green Park ◷ 3.30pm & 5.30pm ⚹ V

## The Savoy (6, C8)  £££

Tea is served in The Savoy's enormous and opulent Thames Foyer accompanied by a pianist and a harpist Monday to Saturday; there's a tea dance on Sunday. Bookings are essential and champagne tea is available. The dress code is smart casual.

✉ Strand WC2
☎ 7836 4343
⊖ Covent Garden, Charing Cross
◷ 3-5.30pm ⚹ V

# entertainment

Choosing how to entertain yourself in London can be daunting with all the options available. Whether you like your culture high or low, your dance in point shoes or heels, your music in strings or sub bass, being sporty or watching others be so, drinking cocktails in an elegant club or a bitter at a pub, London has it all.

London is the world's greatest centre for English-language theatre; it is also a major centre for classical music and ballet.

Day or night all year around, there shouldn't ever be a problem finding something enjoyable to do in London and somewhere to do it.

## Bookings

Most theatre and concert-hall box offices open Monday to Saturday from about 10am to 8pm or 9pm but almost never on Sunday, when most theatres are dark. If a production is sold out you may be able to buy a returned ticket on the day of the performance, although for hit productions you might need to start queuing before returns actually go on sale.

On the day of a performance *only* you can buy half-price tickets for West End productions from the **tkts booth** (6, D5; ⊖ Leicester Square) in the clock tower on the southern side of Leicester Square. It opens Monday to Saturday 10am to 7pm and Sunday noon to 3pm. Payment is by cash or credit/debit card (Visa, MasterCard, American Express, Switch) and a £2.50 commission is added. Be wary of commercial ticket agencies near Leicester Square that advertise half-price tickets without mentioning their high commission charges.

You can book tickets through both Ticketmaster (☎ 7344 4444, e www.ticketmaster.co.uk) or First Call (☎ 7420 0000, e www.first call.co.uk), or directly through the theatre's box office.

Student stand-by tickets are sometimes available an hour before the commencement of a performance. Phone the Student Theatre Line (☎ 7379 8900) for details.

### Read All about It

To find out what's on, buy a copy of the comprehensive entertainment listings magazine *Time Out* (£2.20), which is published every Wednesday (though available Tuesday at most newsagents) and covers the week's events. *Hot Tickets*, free with the *Evening Standard* newspaper on Thursday, is another great source.

Alternatively you can use the London Tourist Board's London Line (☎ 09068 663344; p. 114). Useful entertainment Web sites include the following: e www.clubinlondon.co.uk; e .www.latenightlondon.co.uk; and e www.pubs.com.

Simon Bracken

*Bright lights in Leicester Square*

## SPECIAL EVENTS

Countless festivals and events are held in and around London. Check out the London Tourist Board's bimonthly *Events in London* or its *Annual Events* pamphlet; you can also find events listed on their Web site (**e** www.londontouristboard.com).

**Jan** *London Parade* – on New Year's Day the lord mayor of Westminster leads a parade of 10,000 musicians and street performers from Parliament Square to Berkeley Square

**Late Jan/early Feb** *Chinese New Year* – lion dances in Soho

**Mar** *Oxford & Cambridge Boat Race* – the traditional rowing race on the Thames from Putney to Mortlake

**Late Mar/early Apr** *London Marathon* – a 26-mile (42km) race from Greenwich Park to the Mall via the Isle of Dogs and Victoria Embankment

**May** *Chelsea Flower Show* – at Chelsea Royal Hospital

**June** *Beating Retreat* – military bands and marching in Horse Guards Parade, Whitehall
*Trooping the Colour* – celebrates the Queen's official birthday with parades and pageantry in Horse Guards Parade, Whitehall

**Late June/early Jul** *Wimbledon Lawn Tennis Championships* – runs for two weeks (p. 100)
*City of London Festival* – performances of music, dance, street theatre etc in City churches and squares

**Jul** *Hampton Court Palace International Flower Show* – flowers galore in one of London's finest gardens
*London Pride March & Mardi Gras* – gay and lesbian march from Hyde Park and huge festival in Finsbury Park

**Jul-Sept** *Promenade Concerts* – classical music festival at the Royal Albert Hall (p. 86)

**Aug** *Notting Hill Carnival* – a vast Caribbean carnival (and Europe's biggest outdoor festival) in Notting Hill on the last Sunday and Monday (bank holiday) of the month

**Sept** *London Open House* – general admission, on the third weekend of the month, to some 550 buildings and other sites normally closed to the public
*Pearly Harvest Festival Service* – brings over 100 Pearly Kings and Queens to a service at St Martin-in-the-Fields church (p. 41)

**Oct-Nov** *Dance Umbrella* – British and international companies performing at venues across London for five weeks

**Nov** *Guy Fawkes Day* – 5 Nov is the anniversary of an attempted Catholic coup in 1605, with bonfires and fireworks in parks around the city
*State Opening of Parliament* – the Queen visits Parliament by state coach amid gun salutes
*London Film Festival* – National Film Theatre, South Bank
*Lord Mayor's Show* – on the second Saturday the newly elected lord mayor travels by state coach from Guildhall to the Royal Courts of Justice, amid floats, bands and fireworks
*Remembrance Sunday* – on the second Sunday the Queen and government members lay wreaths at the Cenotaph to honour the dead of the two world wars

**Dec** *Lighting of the Christmas Tree* – Trafalgar Square

# THEATRE

There are some 50 West End theatres that stage a new crop of plays every summer and twice as many off-West End and fringe theatres offering a variety of productions. Here's a selection of more established theatres and some lesser known ones; don't forget to check the programme at the reconstructed Globe Theatre (p. 28).

**Barbican** (3, D12)
The London home of the Royal Shakespeare Company, the Barbican has two auditoriums – the Barbican Theatre and the smaller Pit. It has been staging some exciting productions in recent years.
✉ Silk St EC2 ☎ 7638 8891 e www.barbican .org.uk ⊖ Barbican Ⓢ Barbican £18-28; Pit £12-15 (matinees cheaper) ♿ varies

**Donmar Warehouse** (6, B6) This fine theatre near Covent Garden continues to stage some of the most sought-after productions in town. It's theatre as it was meant to be.
✉ Earlham St WC2 ☎ 7369 1732 e www .donmar-warehouse .com ⊖ Covent Garden Ⓢ £14-242 (stand-by £12)

**King's Head** (2, C10)
Arguably the best 'pub theatre' in London, the King's stages innovative works by young playwrights.
✉ 115 Upper St N1 ☎ 7226 1916 ⊖ Angel Ⓢ £5-14

**Royal Court** (2, H6)
The rebuilt Royal Court has returned home to its two stages on the eastern side of Sloane Square. It tends to favour the new and the anti-establishment.
✉ Sloane Sq SW1 ☎ 7565 5000

e www.royalcourt theatre.com ⊖ Sloane Square Ⓢ £9-24.50 (all seats Mon £5) ♿ varies

**Royal National Theatre** (6, E10)
The nation's flagship theatre has three auditoriums: the Olivier, Lyttleton and Cottesloe. It showcases classics and contemporary

plays, and hosts guest appearances by the world's best young companies.
✉ South Bank SE1 ☎ 7452 3000 e www .nationaltheatre.org.uk ⊖ Waterloo Ⓢ £10-32.50 (less for same-day purchase, standby, restricted view, student, senior and matinee tickets) ♿ varies

## Theatre is Child's Play

The following are four theatres that play to a younger crowd. For other entertainment options for children see pp. 44-45.

**Little Angel Theatre** (2, C11) 14 Dagmar Passage N1 ☎ 7226 1787 ⊖ Angel
**Pleasance Theatre** (2, 49) Carpenter's Mews, North Rd N7 ☎ 7609 1800 ⊖ Caledonian Road
**Polka Theatre** (1, C4) 240 The Broadway SW19 ☎ 8543 4888 ⊖ Wimbledon
**Unicorn Theatre** (2, A10) St Marks Studios, Chillingworth Rd N7 ☎ 7700 0703 ⊖ Holloway Road

Neil Setchfield

*Showing one's face at the Barbican*

# CLASSICAL MUSIC & OPERA

Home to five symphony orchestras, London takes its classical music very seriously. On any given night your choices will range from traditional crowd-pleasers to new music and 'difficult' composers – most to a high standard, in brilliant venues and at reasonable prices. Opera can be more problematic because it's costly to produce and so costly to attend.

### Barbican (3, D12)

The Barbican, not the most delightful of venues, is nevertheless home to the prestigious London Symphony Orchestra.
✉ Silk St EC2 ☎ 7638 8891 ⓔ www.barbican .org.uk) ⊖ Barbican ⓢ £8-30; student & over 60s stand-by £6-9 ♿ varies

### London Coliseum

(6, D6) The home of the English National Opera is a lot more reasonably priced than the Royal Opera House and presents its opera in English. Restricted-view tickets are available from 10am on the day of performance; expect a long queue.
✉ St Martin's La WC1 ☎ 7632 8300 ⓔ www .eno.org ⊖ Leicester Square ⓢ £5-58; students £12; restricted view £3

### Royal Albert Hall

(2, G5) This splendid-looking Victorian concert hall hosts all kinds of performances, including classical music, but the acoustics are terrible. In summer, it stages the Proms, one of the world's biggest classical music festivals.
✉ Kensington Gore SW7 ☎ 7589 8212 ⓔ www.royalalbert hall.com ⊖ South Kensington ⓢ £5-40; Proms £3-70 ♿ varies

### Royal Opera House

(6, B7) Following a £213-million redevelopment, the Opera House has welcomed home the peripatetic Royal Opera and Royal Ballet. Now more proletarian, the renovated Floral Hall opens to the public during the day, with free lunchtime concerts on Monday at 1pm, exhibitions and daily tours.
✉ Covent Garden WC2 ☎ 7304 4000 ⓔ www .royaloperahouse.org ⊖ Covent Garden ⓢ £6-150; midweek matinees £6.50-50 ♿ varies

### South Bank Centre

(6, E9) The Royal Festival Hall, Queen Elizabeth Hall and Purcell Room are three of London's premier venues for classical concerts – from symphonies to chamber groups.
✉ South Bank SE1 ☎ 7960 4242 ⓔ www .rfh.org.uk ⊖ Waterloo ⓢ £5-60 ♿ varies

### Wigmore Hall (3, E3)

This intimate Art Nouveau concert hall is arguably the finest place in London to hear classical music (chamber orchestras, pianists, classical guitarists etc). The Sunday recitals at 11.30am are particularly good and there are Monday lunchtime concerts at 1pm.
✉ 36 Wigmore St W1 ☎ 7935 2141 ⓔ www .wigmore-hall.org.uk ⊖ Bond Street ⓢ £8-23

### The Proms

The real 'Prom' experience at the Royal Albert Hall is queuing for one of the 1000-odd standing (or 'promenading') tickets that go on sale an hour before the beginning of each concert staged from mid-July to mid-September. You can choose to stand in the gallery or the arena; there is a separate queue for each. The Last Night of the Proms is one of those quintessential English affairs: the waving of Union Jacks, drunken chanting of Elgar's *Land of Hope and Glory* and arguments over whether the programme was too modern this year.

The best seats in the house

# BALLET & DANCE

London is home to five major dance companies and a host of small and experimental ones. The Royal Ballet, the best classical ballet company in the land, is based at the Royal Opera House (p. 86); the London Coliseum (p. 86) is another venue for ballet. Visit the London Dance Network's Web site at **e** www.londondance.com for further dance information.

**The Place** (3, B6)
The Place, home to the Richard Alston Dance Company, is one of London's most important addresses for contemporary and experimental dance.
✉ **17 Duke's Rd WC1**
☎ 7387 0031 **e** www.theplace.org ✆ Euston
💲 £5-15

**Sadler's Wells** (3, A10)
Sadler's Wells, which reopened in 1998 after a total refurbishment, attracts contemporary and classical dance troupes from around the world. Its second venue, the West End's **Peacock Theatre** (Portugal St WC2; 6, B9; ✆ Holborn) hosts more popular dance fare and less established companies.
✉ **Rosebery Ave EC1**
☎ 7863 8000 **e** www.sadlers-wells.com
✆ **Angel** 💲 £8.50-40

*Royal Opera House detail*

# COMEDY

London plays host to a number of clubs whose *raison d'être* is comedy; there are even more venues – especially pubs – that set aside specific nights for stand-up routine comedy acts.

**Comedy Café** (3, B14)
There's something for everyone at this colourful and cracking club in Hoxton, just off Shoreditch High St; Wednesday is Try Out Night.
✉ **66-68 Rivington St EC2** ☎ 7739 5706
**e** www.comedycafe.co.uk ✆ Old Street
🕐 Wed-Sat 9pm
💲 £3-12

**Comedy Store** (6, D5)
London's oldest comedy club, now approaching its fourth decade, hosts big acts Tuesday to Sunday.
✉ **1a Oxendon St SW1** ☎ 7344 4444
**e** www.thecomedystore.co.uk ✆ Piccadilly Circus 🕐 Tues-Thurs & Sun 8pm, Fri-Sat 8pm & midnight 💲 £15

**Jongleurs Battersea** (2, K5) This is a branch of a chain that plays it safe but keeps on packing them in. Other branches include:
**Jongleurs Bow Wharf** (221 Grove Rd E3; 2, C15; ✆ Mile End) and **Jongleurs Camden Lock** (11 East Yard NW1; 4, C3; ✆ Camden Town).
✉ **49 Lavender Gardens SW11** ☎ 7564 2500
**e** www.jongleurs.com
🚃 Clapham Junction
🕐 Fri 8.45pm, Sat 7.15pm & 11.15pm
💲 £12-14

*You're guaranteed to have a laugh at Jongleurs.*

# ROCK & POP

London boasts a wide range of rock and pop venues and you can hear everything from megastars at Wembley, Earl's Court or the London Arena and similar hangar-sized arenas to hot new bands at any number of more intimate places around town.

Smaller places with a more club-like atmosphere are worth checking out for local and visiting bands. The times given here are when you can expect to hear music; each venue may be open longer hours as a pub, club etc.

## MEGA-VENUES

**Brixton Academy**
(2, K9) This enormous venue with a great atmosphere is popular with up-and-coming indie and rock groups.
✉ **211 Stockwell Rd SW9** ☎ **7771 2000** [e] **www.brixton-academy.co.uk** ⊖ **Brixton** 🕐 **varies** $ **£10-20**

**Earl's Court Exhibition Centre**
(2, J3) This is one of a handful of venues in London for blockbuster concerts – the type that sell out well in advance – but it has bad acoustics.
✉ **Warwick Rd SW5** ☎ **7385 1200, 0870 903 9033** [e] **www.eco.co.uk** ⊖ **Earl's Court** 🕐 **varies** $ **£5-50**

**The Forum** (4, A4)
Just a few doors down from the Bull and Gate (below), the Forum is an excellent roomy venue for all kinds of rock concerts.
✉ **9-17 Highgate Rd NW5** ☎ **7344 0044** [e] **www.meanfiddler.com** ⊖ **Kentish Town** 🕐 **varies** $ **£5-15**

**Hackney Ocean**
(2, B14) This brand-new multipurpose venue has three auditoriums for 'music making waves' in a renovated old library. Worth the trip for the acoustics alone.
✉ **270 Mare St E8** ☎ **8533 0111** [e] **www.ocean.org.uk** 🚆 **Hackney Central** 🕐 **varies** $ **£1-30**

**Shepherd's Bush Empire** (2, G1)
Once part of BBC TV, now one of London's best venues for top rock, country, soul and indie bands.
✉ **Shepherd's Bush Green W12** ☎ **7771 2000** [e] **www.shepherds-bush-empire.co.uk** ⊖ **Shepherd's Bush** 🕐 **varies** $ **£5-20**

Neil Setchfield

*Earl's Court*

## SMALL BUT LOUD

**Borderline** (6, A5)
This small, relaxed basement venue has a reputation for quality new bands.
✉ **Orange Yard, off Manette St W1** ☎ **7734 2095** [e] **www.borderline.co.uk** ⊖ **Tottenham Court Road** 🕐 **Mon-Fri 8-11pm** $ **£5-10**

**Bull and Gate** (4, A4)
This 'almost Camden' venue is small, smoky and lines up three acts every night of the week.
✉ **389 Kentish Town Rd NW5** ☎ **7485 5358** [e] **www.bullandgate.co.uk** ⊖ **Kentish Town** 🕐 **8.30pm** $ **£3-5**

**Garage** (2, B10)
A good venue for indie rock from both sides of the Atlantic, but the acoustics leave a lot to be desired (and heard).
✉ **20-22 Highbury Cnr N5** ☎ **7607 1818** [e] **www.meanfiddler.com** ⊖ **Highbury & Islington** 🕐 **Mon-Thurs 8pm-midnight, Fri-Sat 8pm-3am** $ **£4-10**

**Rock Garden** (6, C7)
This small basement venue, often packed with tourists, hosts local bands nightly.
✉ **The Piazza, Covent Garden WC2** ☎ **7240 3961** [e] **www.rockgarden.co.uk** ⊖ **Covent Garden** 🕐 **8pm** $ **£4-12**

**Underworld** (4, D4)
Beneath a huge landmark pub called World's End, Underworld is a small venue featuring new bands and has club nights.
✉ **174 Camden High St NW1** ☎ **7482 1932** ⊖ **Camden Town** 🕐 **7pm-3am (nights vary)** $ **£3-12**

# JAZZ

London has always had a thriving jazz scene and, with its recent resurgence thanks to acid-jazz, hip-hop, funk and swing, it's stronger than ever.

**100 Club (6, A4)**
This legendary London venue, once showcasing the Stones and at the centre of the punk revolution, now concentrates on jazz.
✉ 100 Oxford St W1
☎ 7636 0933 e www
.the100club.co.uk
⊖ Oxford Circus
🕐 Mon-Thurs 7.45pm-midnight, Fri 12-3pm & 8.30pm-2am, Sat 7.30pm-1am, Sun 7.30-11.30pm ⓢ £7-15

**Jazz Café (4, D4)**
This is a very trendy restaurant venue with eclectic offerings; it's best to book a table.
✉ 5-7 Parkway NW1
☎ 7916 6060 e www
.jazzcafe.co.uk

⊖ Camden Town
🕐 Mon-Thurs 7pm-1am, Fri-Sat 7pm-2am, Sun 7pm-midnight
ⓢ £10-22

**Pizza Express Jazz Club (6, A4)** This is a small basement venue beneath the main chain restaurant that goes for big names and the mainstream.
✉ 10 Dean St W1
☎ 7439 8722 e www
.pizzaexpress.co.uk
⊖ Tottenham Court Road 🕐 Mon-Thurs & Sun 9pm-11.30pm, Fri-Sat 9pm-midnight
ⓢ £12.50-15

**Ronnie Scott's (6, B5)**
Operating since 1959, this seedy and enjoyable venue attracts big-name talent,

but is expensive if you're not a member (£50/year).
✉ 47 Frith St W1
☎ 7439 0747 e www
.ronniescotts.co.uk
⊖ Leicester Square
🕐 Mon-Sat 8.30pm-3am, Sun 7.30-10.30pm
ⓢ £15-20 (members £5-9; under-26s Mon-Wed £9)

*Jazzy Ronnie Scott's*

# FOLK, TRADITIONAL & WORLD MUSIC

**Africa Centre (6, C7)**
The Africa Centre has African music concerts most Friday nights and other one-offs on Saturday and during the week.
✉ 38 King St WC2
☎ 7836 1973

e www.africacentre
.org.uk ⊖ Covent Garden 🕐 Fri 11.30pm-3am ⓢ £6-8 ⚥ varies

**Cecil Sharp House (4, D2)** The HQ of the English Folk Dance & Song

Society, this is the venue for English folk music (an acquired taste, it must be said). Tuesdays at 8pm offer a mixed (and very esoteric) bag.
✉ 2 Regent's Park Rd NW1 ☎ 7485 2206
⊖ Camden Town
🕐 7pm (nights vary) ⓢ £3-6 ⚥ varies

**Swan (2, K9)**
Traditional Irish bands play every night in this large pub directly opposite Stockwell tube station.
✉ 215 Clapham Rd SW9 ☎ 7978 9778
e www.theswan
stockwell.com
⊖ Stockwell
🕐 9.30pm ⓢ £1.50-6

*Glasses lined up at the ready*

# CINEMAS

During the 1950s and 60s many of London's great Art Deco cinema houses shut down. The first multiplex cinemas appeared in the late 80s and they just keep on coming. Offering a wider choice of films at one site and more comfortable seating, they can also be expensive and show mostly mainstream American fare. Full-price tickets cost £8 to £10 for a first-run film; an afternoon weekday session and anytime on Monday is usually cheaper (£4.50-5).

**Electric Cinema** (2, E2)
An ambitious refurbishment of this Edwardian building, the oldest purpose-built cinema in the UK, has created a new three-storey annexe with 200 comfy seats, a bar and a bookshop.
✉ **191 Portobello Rd W11** ☎ **7229 8688** ⊖ **Notting Hill** ♿ **varies**

**National Film Theatre** (6, E10)
The modern National Film Theatre, built in 1958, screens some 2000 films a year; for details check *Time Out*. It also hosts the London Film Festival in November, a cinematic cornucopia of less regularly screened gems.
✉ **South Bank SE1** ☎ **7928 3232** e **www .bfi.org.uk/nft** ⊖ **Waterloo, Embankment** ♿ **varies**

**Prince Charles Cinema** (6, C5)
Far and away central London's cheapest cinema (£2-3.50), the Prince Charles shows several films daily and usually has a range of new releases, foreign and old films on the programme.
✉ **Leicester Pl WC2** ☎ **7437 8181** e **www .princecharlescinema .com** ⊖ **Leicester Square** ♿ **varies**

## Fresh Air Culture
London can't boast the world's best weather, but that doesn't mean you're limited to cinema outings or other indoor pursuits. When the sun shines, take in a Shakespearean play or a musical at the **Open Air Theatre** in Regent's Park (3, B2; ☎ 7486 2431; e www.open-air-theatre.org.uk). Another summer's day highlight is to see a classical concert in the grounds of **Kenwood House** (p. 36).

*Think big at the National Film Theatre.*

# DANCE CLUBS

Though the majority of London's pubs still close at 11pm, there are clubs where you can carry on partying, although you'll have to pay to get in and the drinks are always fairly expensive.

Dress can be smart (ie, no suits) or casual; the more outrageous you look the better chance you have of getting in. But in the end, that all depends, of course, on the gorilla at the door.

**333** (3, B14)
This is a distressed-looking venue in Hoxton with everything from breakbeats and techno to funk.
✉ 333 Old St EC1
☎ 7739 5949 ⊖ Old Street ⏰ Mon-Thurs 8pm-2am, Fri-Sat 10pm-5am Sun 10pm-4am

**93 Fleet Street** (3, C15)
This former warehouse with several levels in the heart of Bangla Town has lots of Asian underground and electronic sounds in its Bad Magic Main Room and Nucamp Balearic Bar.
✉ 150 Brick La E2
☎ 7247 3293 ⊖ Shoreditch, Aldgate East
⏰ Mon-Wed 6pm-11pm, Thurs-Sat 8pm-2am, Sun 12-10.30pm

**Aquarium** (3, B13)
Aquarium is a converted gym with its own cool pool, spa and restaurant. The club is transformed into an underwater paradise for Saturday night's 'Big Fish'.
✉ 256-260 Old St EC1
☎ 7251 6136 ⊖ Old Street ⏰ Fri-Sun 10pm-4am

**Bagleys Studios** (2, C9)
Bagleys is a huge converted warehouse with five dance floors, four bars and an outside area in summer; it hosts big weekend parties too.
✉ King's Cross Freight Depot, York Way N1

☎ 7278 2777 ⊖ King's Cross St Pancras ⏰ Fri 9pm-6am, Sat 10pm-7am

**Camden Palace** (4, E5)
This multilevel monster of a place gets thick with sweaty boppers and laser lights.
✉ 1a Camden High St NW1 ☎ 7387 0428
⊖ Mornington Crescent ⏰ Tues 10pm-2.30am, Thurs 8pm-3am, Fri 10pm-6am, Sat 10pm-7am

**The Cross** (2, C9)
Hidden under the arches off York Way, newly renovated and with brilliant DJs, this is one of London's leading venues. Friday is 'Fiction', with soulful funk and garage.
✉ Goods Way Depot, York Way N1 ☎ 7837 0828 ⊖ King's Cross St Pancras ⏰ Fri-Sat 10.30pm-5am, Sun 10.30pm-4am

**Dogstar** (2, K9)
Dogstar is as casual as you'd expect from a converted pub, so dressing to kill is not imperative. It houses big parties at weekends.
✉ 389 Coldharbour La SW9 ☎ 7733 7515
⊖ Brixton ⏰ Mon-Thurs noon-1am, Fri-Sat noon-4am

**Dust** (3, C10)
This is a classy DJ bar open late at weekends.
✉ 27 Clerkenwell Rd

EC1 ☎ 7490 0537
⊖ Farringdon ⏰ Thurs noon-1am, Fri-Sat noon-3am, Sun 12-11pm

> ## It Costs to Club
> Admission can be hefty, varying from £2 to £5 between Sunday and Thursday and £6 to £12 on Friday and Saturday, but not all clubs charge a cover. Drinks are likely to cost at least £3 a pop, and you'll have to leave at least £10 in your pocket for the cab fare home.

*A raving mad clubber*

**Emporium** (6, C3)
Very popular with the beautiful set, tourists and assorted trash, the Emporium is at the posh end of the scale.
✉ 62 Kingly St W1
☎ 7734 3190
⊖ Oxford Circus
⏰ Thurs-Fri 10pm-4am, Sat 9pm-5am

## The End (6, A7)

A postmodern club with an industrial decor on a West End backstreet. For serious clubbers who like their dance music at the hard end of the scale.

✉ **18 West Central St WC1** ☎ **7419 9199** ⊖ **Holborn** ◷ **Mon 10pm-3am, Thurs 10pm-4am, Fri-Sat 10pm-7am**

## Fabric (3, C11)

This feather in Clerkenwell's well-plumed cap boasts three dance floors in a converted meat cold-store, a 24-hour music licence and a capacity for 2500 groovers.

✉ **77a Charterhouse St EC1** ☎ **7336 8898, 7490 0444** ⊖ **Farringdon** ◷ **Fri & Sun 10pm-5am, Sat 10pm-7am**

## The Fridge (2, K9)

The Fridge offers a wide variety of club nights in an excellent venue that is not too big, not too small. It's still one of the best clubs in London.

✉ **1 Town Hall Pde, Brixton Hill SW2** ☎ **7326 5100** ⊖ **Brixton** ◷ **Fri-Sat 10pm-6am**

## Hanover Grand (6, B2)

A split-level venue with a strict dress code but worth queuing for. Friday night is 'Independence', with US garage and house.

✉ **6 Hanover St W1** ☎ **7499 7977** ⊖ **Oxford Circus** ◷ **Wed 10pm-3.30am, Thurs-Fri 10pm-4am, Sat 10pm-4.30am**

## Mass (2, K9)

This appropriately named club in a disused church with vaulted ceilings, pews and frescoes, resounds to hard house, trance and a bit of industrial.

✉ **St Matthew's Church, Brixton Hill SW2** ☎ **7737 1016** ⊖ **Brixton** ◷ **Thurs 10pm-2am, Fri 10pm-6am, Sat 9pm-6am**

## Ministry of Sound (2, G11)

This cavernous place, arguably London's most famous club (though well past its finest hour, they say), attracts hard-core clubbers and boozers with its phenomenal sound system.

✉ **103 Gaunt St SE1** ☎ **7378 6528** e **www .ministryofsound.co.uk** ⊖ **Elephant & Castle** ◷ **Fri 10.30pm-6am, Sat 12-9am**

## Notting Hill Arts Club (2, F3)

A cosy, groovy club whose jewel in the crown is Sunday night's 'Lazy Dog'.

✉ **21 Notting Hill Gate W11** ☎ **7460 4459** ⊖ **Notting Hill Gate** ◷ **Tues-Sun 6pm-1am**

## Turnmills (3, C10)

This large, long-running venue does big weekend parties, including a gay one called 'Trade'.

✉ **63 Clerkenwell Rd EC1** ☎ **7250 3409** ⊖ **Farringdon** ◷ **Tues 6pm-midnight, Fri 10.30pm-7.30am, Sat 9pm-1pm, Sun 10pm-6am**

## Velvet Room (6, A5)

The Room is an intimate, low-lit club swathed in plush red velvet.

✉ **143 Charing Cross Rd WC2** ☎ **7439 4655** ⊖ **Tottenham Court Road** ◷ **Mon & Thurs 10pm-3am, Tues 10.30pm-3am, Wed 10pm-2.30am, Fri-Sat 10pm-4am**

## Club Is in the Air

Clubs can change from night to night, depending on the DJ and the targeted crowd – techno heads, gays, salsa fans etc. General opening times are given here, but for specific theme and time information, see *Time Out* or flyers at pubs and record shops around Soho and Hoxton.

*Getting mixed up to the beats*

Simon Bracken

# PUBS & BARS

Pubs are perhaps the most distinctive contribution the English have made to social life, and little can compare to a good one. What that constitutes – beyond a wide range of beer and real ales – is very subjective and almost indefinable: a warm welcome, a sense of bonhomie, the feel of a 'local'. The following includes some of our favourites; for more suggestions look for the *Time Out Pubs & Bars* guide (£5.99) or check out **e** www.pubs.com.

### AKA (6, A7)

This popular late-hour DJ bar joins together with its neighbour, the End (p. 92) till 7am on Saturday.
⊠ **18 West Central St W1** ☎ **7836 0110** ⊖ **Holborn** ⊘ **Mon 6pm-midnight, Tues 6pm-midnight, Wed-Fri 6pm-3am, Sat 7pm-3am**

### The Anchor Bankside

(3, G12) This 18th-century place just east of the Globe Theatre has superb views across the Thames from its terrace and is the nicest (and most popular) riverside pub in London.
⊠ **34 Park St SE1** ☎ **7407 1577** ⊖ **London Bridge** ⚲ **yes (restaurant only)**

### Bar Vinyl (4, D4)

This laid-back bar with an LP theme has a DJ spinning disks most nights.
⊠ **6 Inverness St NW1** ☎ **7681 7898** ⊖ **Camden Town**

### Beach Blanket Babylon (2, F3)

This crazy place boasts extraordinary Gothic decor and is great for observing Notting Hill trendies by day and night.
⊠ **45 Ledbury Rd W11** ☎ **7229 2907** ⊖ **Notting Hill Gate** ⊘ **Mon-Sat 12-11pm, Sun 12-10.30pm**

### Bug Bar (2, K9)

In the crypt of an old Methodist church, this convivial place hosts everything from bands and DJs to comics.
⊠ **St Matthew's Church, Brixton Hill SW2** ☎ **7738 3184** ⊖ **Brixton** ⊘ **Mon-Sat 7pm-2am, Sun 5pm-10.30pm**

### Cantaloupe (3, B14)

This was the first kid on the block when Hoxton and Shoreditch started to get trendy, and it still manages to feel arty enough without being overwhelming. There's a decent restaurant here.
⊠ **35-43 Charlotte Rd EC2** ☎ **7613 4411** ⊖ **Old Street** ⊘ **Mon-Fri 11am-midnight, Sat noon-midnight, Sun 12-11.30pm** ⚲ **yes (restaurant only)**

### The Captain Kidd

(2, G14) The Kidd, with its large windows, fine beer garden and mock scaffold recalling the hanging of the eponymous pirate in 1701, is a favourite riverside pub on the northern bank of the Thames.
⊠ **108 Wapping High St E1** ☎ **7480 5759** ⊖ **Wapping**

### The Churchill Arms

(2, G3) This traditional English pub is renowned for its Winston memorabilia, chamber pots suspended from a great height (go figure) and decent Thai food served in a lovely conservatory.
⊠ **119 Kensington Church St W8** ☎ **7727 4242** ⊖ **Notting Hill Gate**

### The Coach & Horses

(6, B5) The Coach is a small, busy pub with a regular clientele of soaks, writers (would-be and otherwise) and the odd tourist.
⊠ **29 Greek St W1** ☎ **7437 5920** ⊖ **Leicester Square**

### Keeping Irregular Hours

Pubs and bars can have complex opening hours in London. In general, they are open Monday to Saturday from 11am to 11pm and on Sunday from midday to 10.30pm. In this chapter, we have only provided those opening hours that differ from the norm.

Simon Bracken

*Half full or half empty?*

**The Counting House**
(3, E13) This award-winning pub in the former headquarters of NatWest attracts suits on the loose after the markets shut. Like most City pubs, it closes at weekends.
✉ 50 Cornhill EC3
☎ 7283 7123 ⊖ Bank
⏲ Mon-Fri 11am-11pm

**The Engineer** (4, D2)
A pretty Victorian place converted into a highly successful pub and gastro-pub restaurant upstairs, the Engineer attracts a groovy north London set.
✉ 65 Gloucester Ave NW1 ☎ 7722 0950
⊖ Chalk Farm ⏲ Mon-Sat 9am-11pm, Sun 9am-10.30pm

## The Name Game

These days really traditional pubs are thin on the ground in London; in many areas spruced-up chain pubs – look for the words 'slug', 'lettuce', 'rat', 'firkin', 'parrot' and 'moon' in their names – have taken over the role of the 'local'. American-style bars and Irish pubs are also very popular.

*The Famous Angel*

**The Famous Angel**
(2, G14) The Angel is a riverside pub dating from the 15th century; Captain Cook supposedly prepared for his trip to Australia from here.
✉ 101 Bermondsey Wall East SE16 ☎ 7237 3608 ⊖ Rotherhithe
♿ yes (dining area only)

**The Fire Station**
(3, H9) This immensely popular pub and gastropub is in a part of town that was once a nightlife and culinary desert.
✉ 150 Waterloo Rd SE1 ☎ 7620 2226
⊖ Waterloo ♿

**The Flask** (1, B5)
The Hampstead Flask is a friendly local that's handy for the tube, with high ceilings, Victorian trimmings and real ale. Not to be confused with its older sister pub across the heath also called **The Flask** (77 Highgate West Hill N6; 2, B5; ⊖ Highgate), which is a maze of snugs.
✉ 14 Flask Walk NW3 ☎ 7435 4580 ⊖ Hampstead ♿ yes (till 7pm)

**The George Inn**
(3, G13) The George is a rare bird indeed – a National Trust pub. It's London's last surviving galleried coaching inn dating from 1676 and is mentioned in Charles Dickens' *Little Dorrit*. Here too is the site of the Tabard Inn (thus Talbot Yard), where the pilgrims in Chaucer's *Canterbury Tales* gathered before setting out.
✉ Talbot Yard, 77 Borough High St SE1 ☎ 7407 2056
⊖ Borough, London Bridge

*A snippet of pub life*

Simon Bracken

**Ion Bar** (2, E2)
This is a very large and popular Afro-Caribbean bar, but a bit of a fishbowl with its huge front windows.
✉ 161-165 Ladbroke Grove W11 ☎ 8960 1702 ⊖ Ladbroke Grove ⏲ Mon-Fri 5pm-midnight, Sat-Sun noon-midnight ♿ yes (restaurant only)

**The King's Head & Eight Bells** (2, J5)
This attractive corner pub, pleasantly hung with flower baskets in summer, has a wide range of beers and was a favourite of the painter Whistler and the writer Carlyle, who lived at 24 Cheyne Row.
✉ 50 Cheyne Walk SW3 ☎ 7352 1820
⊖ Sloane Square
⏲ Mon-Sat 12-11pm, Sun 12-10.30pm

**The Lamb & Flag**
(6, C7) This pleasantly unchanged pub is everyone's 'find' in Covent Garden and is thus always jammed. It was once known as the Bucket of Blood – either because of the fighters who favoured it as a local or because the poet John Dryden was attacked outside in 1679

Neil Setchfield

for having written less-than-complimentary verses about King Charles II's mistress, the duchess of Portsmouth.

✉ 33 Rose St WC2
☎ 7497 9504
⊖ Covent Garden ♿

**Liquid Lab** (3, C13)
This ultra-cool watering station with a medical/dental theme defies description (but you'll certainly need one for cocktails such as Blood Clot and Sperm Bank).

✉ 20 City Rd EC1
☎ 7920 0372 ⊖ Old Street ◷ Mon-Fri 11am-11pm

**The Museum Tavern**
(3, D6) After a hard day's work in the British Museum Reading Room, Karl Marx used to repair to this narrow pub, where you too can sup your pint and reflect on dialectical materialism if so inclined.

✉ 49 Great Russell St WC1 ☎ 7242 8987
⊖ Holborn

**O'Hanlon's** (3, B9)
Come to O'Hanlon's for house-brewed beer and an eclectic range of distressed seats and sofas under a skylight.

✉ 8 Tysoe St EC1
☎ 7278 7630 ⊖ Angel
$ 11am-11pm

**Princess Louise** (3, D7)
This Grade II-listed pub has some smashing Victorian decor, with fine tiles, etched mirrors, plasterwork and a stunning central bar.

✉ 208 High Holborn WC1 ☎ 7405 8816
⊖ Holborn ◷ Mon-Fri 11am-11pm, Sat 12-11pm ♿

**The Salisbury** (6, C6)
Brave the crowds at this centrally located pub established in 1898 just to see the beautifully etched and engraved windows and other Victorian features that have somehow escaped the developer's hand.

✉ 90 St Martin's La WC2 ☎ 7836 5863
⊖ Leicester Square

**Scruffy Murphy's**
(6, C4) This favourite little place is a relatively authentic Irish pub, with brogues, Guinness and drunks.

✉ 15 Denman St W1
☎ 7437 1540
⊖ Piccadilly Circus

**Three Kings of Clerkenwell** (3, C10)
A friendly pub a stone's throw from Clerkenwell Green, it's festooned with papier-mâché models, including a giant rhino head above the fireplace.

✉ 7 Clerkenwell Close EC1 ☎ 7253 0483
⊖ Farringdon ◷ Mon-Fri 12-11pm, Sat 7.30pm-11pm

**Trafalgar Tavern**
(5, C3) This cavernous pub, with big windows looking on to the Thames and the ill-fated Millennium Dome, is steeped in history. It stands above the site of

## Good for What Ales You

In public houses you can order wine or even a cocktail, but the *raison d'être* of 'pubs' is to serve beer – be it lager, ale or stout in a pint (570mL) or half-pint (285mL) glass. The term lager refers to the amber-coloured bottom-fermented beverage found the world over. In general, lagers are highly carbonated, of medium hop flavour and drunk cool or cold. Ale is a top-fermented beer whose flavours can run the gamut from subtle to robust. They can be very slightly gassy or completely still, usually have a strong hop flavour and are drunk at slightly above room temperature. There are dozens of varieties but when in doubt just ask for 'a bitter' and you'll be served the house ale.

*Pulling in the punters with a perfectly poured pint*

the old Placentia Palace where Henry VIII was born. Dickens knocked back a few here and prime ministers Gladstone and Disraeli used to dine on the pub's celebrated whitebait.
**✉ Park Row SE10 ☎ 8858 2437 🚆 DLR Cutty Sark 👶**

**The Warrington Hotel** (2, D4) This former hotel and brothel is now an ornate Art Nouveau pub with character aplenty and a very laid-back atmosphere. There's courtyard seating and a Thai-run (gratefully) Thai restaurant upstairs.
**✉ 93 Warrington Crescent W9 ☎ 7266 3134 ⊖ Warwick Ave 👶**

**Ye Olde Mitre** (3, D10) Founded in 1546, this is one of London's oldest and most historic pubs, but the 18th-century-sized rooms can be a bit tight for 21st-century punters.
**✉ 1 Ely Court, off Hatton Garden EC1 ☎ 7405 4751 ⊖ Chancery Lane 🕒 Mon-Fri 11am-11pm**

*A taste of pub grub*

# OPEN ALL HOURS

London might party hard and late in its dance clubs (pp. 91-92) but elsewhere it can feel like an early-to-bed kind of place. Still, there are options, provided you know where to look. (See p. 83 for a guide to the pricing symbols.)

## CAFES & RESTAURANTS

**1997 Special Zone** (6, C5) Head here if you've got a craving for Peking duck or comforting soup noodles at 4am or later/earlier.
**✉ 19 Wardour St W1 ☎ 7734 2868 ⊖ Piccadilly Circus or Leicester Square 🕒 24hrs $ ££**

Simon Bracken
*Back to the 50s at Bar Italia*

**Bar Italia** (6, B5) This great favourite has wonderful 1950s decor. It's always packed and buzzing (from the caffeine, no doubt).
**✉ 22 Frith St W1 ☎ 7437 4520 ⊖ Leicester Square 🕒 Mon-Sat 24hrs, Sun 7am-4am**

**Mezzo** (6, B4) Another Conran venture that attracts a late-night media crowd and hangers-on, the basement Mezzo, which serves Modern European fare, is massive. More casual and cheaper is the ground floor Mezzonine, an Asian fusion place.
**✉ 100 Wardour St W1 ☎ 7314 4000 [e] www.conran.com ⊖ Piccadilly Circus 🕒 Mezzo: Mon-Thurs 6pm-12.30am, Fri-Sat 6pm-2.30am, Sun 6pm-10.30pm; Mezzonine: Mon-Thurs 5.30pm-1am, Fri-Sat 5.30pm-3am $ Mezzo £££; Mezzonine ££**

**Old Compton Café** (6, B5) A friendly, sometimes frantic cafe in the middle of Soho offering an endless choice of sandwiches.
**✉ 34 Old Compton St W1 ☎ 7439 3309 ⊖ Tottenham Court Road, Leicester Square 🕒 24hrs $ £**

**Tinseltown** (3, C11) This American-style basement diner in Clerkenwell serves average pizza, pasta, burgers and grills round the clock.
**✉ 44-46 St John's St EC1 ☎ 7689 2424 ⊖ Farringdon or Barbican 🕒 24hrs $ ££**

**Vingt-Quatre** (2, J4) The '80' is an extremely popular place with a proper

menu at lunch and dinner but offering more basic stuff after midnight (when the bar closes).
✉ **325 Fulham Rd SW10 ☎ 7376 7224 ⊖ South Kensington, then bus 14 or 211 🕐 24hrs $ ££**

## PUBS & BARS

**Bar Rumba** (6, C4)
This is a small club in the heart of Soho with a loyal following. Tuesday is a Rumba Pa'ti, Saturday is Garage City and Sunday is Bubblin' Over, with ghetto soul and rap.
✉ **36 Shaftesbury Ave W1 ☎ 7287 2715 ⊖ Piccadilly Circus 🕐 Mon-Thurs 5pm-3.30am, Fri 5pm-4am, Sat 7pm-6am, Sun 8pm-1am**

**Charlie Wright's International Bar**
(2, D12) This is a useful address if you want to carry on after usual pub hours. The clientele is a mixed bag (as far as we can remember).
✉ **45 Pitfield St N1 ☎ 7490 8345 ⊖ Old Street 🕐 Mon-Wed noon-1am, Thurs-Sun noon-2am 👶 till 7pm**

Neil Setchfield
*Give Havana a whirl.*

**Cuba Libre** (2, C10)
This lively bar at the back of a fairly ordinary restaurant has great cocktails, samba for days and stays open late at weekends.
✉ **72 Upper St N1 ☎ 7354 9998 ⊖ Angel 🕐 Mon-Thurs 11am-11pm, Fri-Sat 11am-2am, Sun 11am-10.30pm 👶 restaurant only**

**Havana** (2, K3)
You could hardly miss this place even if you did blink: it's a neon-lit blue and ochre tiled cocktail bar/restaurant with zebra-striped and leopard-spotted seating.
✉ **490 Fulham Rd SW6 ☎ 7381 5005 ⊖ Fulham Broadway 🕐 Mon-Thurs 5pm-2am, Fri-Sat noon-2am, Sun 12-10.30pm**

**The O Bar** (6, C4)
This upbeat bar has two main drinking floors with a DJ downstairs every night. There is another branch (3, C3; ⊖ Baker Street, Regent's Park) at 21a Devonshire St W1.
✉ **83-85 Wardour St W1 ☎ 7437 3490 ⊖ Piccadilly Circus 🕐 Mon-Sat 5pm-3am, Sun 4pm-10.30pm**

# GAY & LESBIAN LONDON

London's bars and clubs cater for every predilection, but there's a growing trend towards mixed gay and straight clubs. Check the press for men- or women-only nights. Much of the activity is centred in Soho but you'll find pubs, cafes and clubs in every direction.

## CAFES

**Balans** (6, B5)
Balans is a moderately priced, continental-style cafe. A branch called **Balans West** (5, H2; ⊖ Earl's Court) is at 239 Old Brompton Rd SW5.
✉ **60 Old Compton St W1 ☎ 7437 5212 ⊖ Tottenham Court Road 🕐 Mon-Thurs 8am-5am, Fri-Sat 8am-6am, Sun 8am-2am $ ££**

**First Out** (6, A5)
This long-established, friendly lesbian-gay cafe serves vegetarian food.
✉ **52 St Giles High St WC2 ☎ 7240 8042 ⊖ Tottenham Court**

**Road 🕘 Mon-Sat 10am-11pm, Sun 11am-10.30pm $ £**

**Freedom** (6, B4)
Around the corner from Balans, you'll find this upbeat place serving food and drink to a mixed clientele.
**✉ 60-66 Wardour St W1 ☎ 7734 0071 ⊖ Piccadilly Circus 🕘 Mon 11am-3am $ £**

## PUBS, BARS & CLUBS

**The Astoria** (6, A5)
This dark, sweaty and atmospheric club has G.A.Y ('good as you') nights throughout the week, including Thursday's Music Factory and Friday's Camp Attack.
**✉ 157 Charing Cross Rd WC2 ☎ 7434 9592, 7434 6963 [e] www.g-a-y.co.uk ⊖ Tottenham Court Road 🕘 Mon-Thurs 10.30pm-4am, Fri 11pm-4am, Sat 10.30pm-4.30am**

**Candy Bar** (6, B5)
The venue of choice among the London clitorati, Candy Bar opens till late most nights and is always packed.
**✉ 23-24 Bateman St W1 ☎ 7494 4041 [e] www.candybar.easynet.co.uk ⊖ Tottenham Court Road 🕘 Mon-Tues 5pm-1am, Wed-Fri 5pm-3am, Sat 4pm-3am, Sun 5pm-midnight**

**Central Station**
(2, C9) This ever-popular place has a bar and club with special one-nighters and the UK's only gay sports bar.
**✉ 37 Wharfdale Rd N1 ☎ 7278 3294 [e] www.centralstation.co.uk ⊖ King's Cross St Pancras 🕘 Mon-Wed 5pm-2am, Thurs 5pm-3am, Fri 5pm-4am, Sat 1pm-4am, Sun 1pm-midnight**

**Heaven** (6, E7)
A long-standing and perennially popular gay club with some mixed nights.
**✉ Under the Arches, Villiers St WC2 ☎ 7930 2020 [e] www.heaven-london.com ⊖ Charing Cross, Embankment 🕘 Mon & Wed 10.30pm-3am, Fri 10.30pm-5am, Sat 10.30pm-6am**

**Rupert Street** (6, C4)
Situated on a corner with large glass windows for looking, being looked at, looking at being looked at etc, Rupert Street is among London's trendiest gay bars.
**✉ 50 Rupert St W1 ☎ 7292 7141 ⊖ Piccadilly Circus 🕘 Mon-Sat 12-11pm, Sun 12-10.30pm**

**The White Swan**
(2, F15) If you're interested in barrow boys (some real, most *faux*) with buzz cuts, check out the East End's friendliest, cruisiest pub/club.
**✉ 556 Commercial Rd E14 ☎ 7780 9870 🚆 DLR Limehouse 🕘 Mon 9pm-1am, Tues-Thurs 9pm-2am, Fri-Sat 9pm-3am, Sun 5.30pm-midnight**

### Gay & Lesbian News

The best starting point is to pick up the free *Pink Paper*, a relatively serious publication in a new magazine format; *Boyz*, which is geared more towards entertainment; and the similar *QX*. All are available from gay cafes, bars and clubs. Magazines such as *Gay Times* (£2.95) and the lesbian *Diva* (£2.25) also have listings. The four-page gay section of *Time Out* is another excellent source of information. Useful Web sites include [e] www.rainbownetwork.com for gay men and [e] www.gingerbeer.co.uk for lesbians.

*Taking it easy at Rupert Street*

# SPECTATOR SPORTS

## Athletics

Athletics meetings attracting major international and domestic stars take place regularly throughout the summer at the **Crystal Palace National Sports Centre** (Ledrington Rd SE19; 1, C5; ☎ 8778 0131; |e| www.crystalpalace .co.uk; Crystal Palace).

## Cricket

Despite the average performance of the England team, cricket is still a popular game. Test matches take place at **Lord's** (St John's Wood Rd NW8; 2, D5; ☎ 7432 1066; |e| www.lords.org; ⊖ St John's Wood) and the **Oval** (Kennington Oval SE11; 2, J9; ☎ 7582 7764; |e| www.surreyccc.co.uk; ⊖ Oval). Tickets are pricey (£ 20-50) and tend to go fast; you're better off looking out for a county fixture (£8-10) at either ground. The season runs from April to September.

## Football

There are a dozen league teams in London; half of them enjoy the big time of the Premier League. So any weekend of the season, from August to mid-May, quality football is just a tube ride away, if you're able to get hold of a ticket.

North-west London's **Wembley Stadium**, where the English national side has traditionally played international matches and the FA Cup Final has taken place in mid-May, closed in 2000. The plan was to replace it with a new 80,000-seat national stadium, but at the time of writing everything was on hold, and major football matches were being played at stadiums outside London.

### Just the Ticket

Phone for match details/credit-card bookings:

**Arsenal** ☎ 7704 4000/7413 3366 |e| www.arsenal.com
**Charlton Athletic** ☎ 8333 4000/8333 4010 |e| www.charlton-athletic.co.uk
**Chelsea** ☎ 7385 5545/7386 7799 |e| www.chelseafc.co.uk
**Fulham** ☎ 7893 8383/7384 4710 |e| www.fulhamfc.co.uk
**Tottenham Hotspur** ☎ 8365 5000/08700 112222 |e| www.spurs.co.uk
**West Ham** ☎ 8548 2748/8548 2700 |e| www.westhamunited.co.uk

Neil Setchfield

*The East Stand of Arsenal's Highbury Stadium, home to the club since 1913*

## Rugby Union & Rugby League

South-west London is the focus for rugby union, with teams such as the Harlequins, Wasps and London Welsh playing from August to May. Each year between January and March, England, Scotland, Wales, Ireland, France and Italy compete in the Six Nations Rugby Union Championship. The shrine of English rugby union is **Twickenham Rugby Stadium** (Rugby Rd, Twickenham; 1, B4; ☎ 8892 2000, ℮ www.rfu.com; ⊖ Hounslow East, then bus 281 or ⓠ Twickenham).

The **London Broncos** (The Valley, Floyd Rd SE7; 1, B5; ☎ 8853 8001, ℮ www.londonbroncos.co.uk; ⓠ Charlton) is the only rugby league side in southern England.

## Racing

There are plenty of top-quality horse racecourses within striking distance of London, including **Ascot** (☎ 01344-622211, ℮ www.ascot.co.uk) in Berkshire and **Epsom** (☎ 01372-470047, ℮ www.epsomderby.co.uk) in Surrey. The flat-racing season runs from April to September.

Looking for a cheap (£1.50-5 for a 12-race meeting) and thrilling night at the races? Consider 'going to the dogs'. There's greyhound racing at **Catford Stadium** (Adenmore Rd SE6; 5, E4; ☎ 8690 8000; ⓠ Catford Bridge) and **Walthamstow Stadium** (Chingford Rd E4; ☎ 8531 4255, ℮ www.wsgreyhound.co.uk; ⓠ Highams Park).

## Tennis

The All England Lawn Tennis Championships have been taking place in late June/early July since 1877 at **Wimbledon** (Church Rd SW19; 1, C4; ☎ 8944 1066, 8946 2244; ℮ www.wimbledon.org; ⊖ Southfields, Wimbledon Park). But the queues, exorbitant prices, limited ticket availability and cramped conditions may have you thinking that Wimbledon is just, well, a racket. Some seats for Centre Court and Court Nos 1 & 2 are sold on the day of play but queues are painfully long.

The nearer to the finals it is, the higher the prices. Prices for the outside courts cost less than £10 and are reduced again after 5pm. There's a public ballot (1 September to 31 December) for the best seats for the next year. To try your luck, send a stamped self-addressed envelope to: All England Lawn Tennis Club, PO Box 98, Church Rd, Wimbledon SW19 5AE. For tours of the Wimbledon Lawn Tennis Museum, see page 37.

*Anyone for tennis?*

David Tomlinson

# places to stay

Where you choose to stay in London will have an effect on the kind of time you have in the city. You want ethnic London? Stay in Notting Hill or Brixton. If your idea of the British capital is one of stately Georgian houses, Regency crescents and private parks in the centre of leafy squares, book a place in Chelsea or South Kensington. Culture vultures and/or those with literary aspirations should choose a place in Kensington, Bloomsbury or even Fitzrovia. You want workaday London with barrow boys, girls in white-heeled shoes and Cockney accents? Choose somewhere in the East End. And if you want to hang out with your 'mites', Earl's Court (aka Kangaroo Valley) or Shepherd's Bush is for you.

Simon Bracken

### Room Rates

These categories indicate the cost per night of a standard double room in high season.

| | |
|---|---|
| Deluxe | from £230 |
| Top End | £130-229 |
| Mid-Range | £70-129 |
| Budget | under £70 |

Unfortunately, wherever you stay accommodation in London is going to take a great wad out of your pocket. B&Bs and guesthouses can be the cheapest option, though the latter, often just large converted houses with a few rooms, can be less personal. Demand can outstrip supply – especially at the bottom end of the market – so it's worth booking at least a night or two before arriving, particularly in summer (when rates rise by up to 25%). Single rooms are in short supply in London, and places are reluctant to let a double room to one person without charging a hefty supplement. Before you travel, it's worth checking whether transport and accommodation packages are cheaper than making arrangements on arrival.

Another problem can be quality – even at the mid-range. The bulk of readers' letters sent to Lonely Planet about London are complaints about the quality and cleanliness of hostels, guesthouses and some B&Bs, 'fauna' in the rooms and the rudeness of staff. Please read the descriptions found in this chapter carefully and make your choices.

### Booking Services

Free same-day accommodation bookings can be made at most tourist information centres (p. 115). Telephone or email bookings (☎ 7932 2020; e book@londontourisboard.co.uk) cost £5. Also worth a try are:

**British Hotel Reservation Centre** – Victoria Station (☎ 0800 282888; e www.bhronline.com; £3)

**First Option** (£5 per booking) – there are kiosks at the Britain Visitor Centre (p. 115); Euston (☎ 7388 7435), King's Cross (☎ 7837 5681), Victoria (☎ 7828 4646) and Gatwick Airport (☎ 01293-529372) train stations; and South Kensington tube station (☎ 7581 9766)

**B&B bookings** (usually for a minimum of three nights and 5% booking fee) – London Homestead Services (☎ 8949 4455; e www.lhslondon.com), Bed & Breakfast Reservations Service (☎ 01 491-578803) and London Bed & Breakfast Agency (☎ 7586 2768; e www.londonbb.com)

**Host & Guest Service** – (☎ 7385 9922; e www.host-guest.co.uk) books B&Bs and student accommodation

# DELUXE

### Brown's (6, D3)

This stunning 5-star, 118-room hotel was created in 1837 from 11 adjoining houses and is London's longest-operating deluxe hotel. It was also the first hotel in London to have a lift, a telephone and electric lighting.

⌧ **30 Albemarle St W1**
☎ **7493 6020; fax 7493 9381** e **browns@ brownshotel.com; www.brownshotel.com** ↔ **Green Park** ✗ **Restaurant 1837, The Drawing Room (afternoon tea)**

### Claridge's (3, F3)

Claridge's, a cherished reminder of a bygone era, is one of London's greatest 5-star hotels. Many of the Art Deco features of the public areas and 203 rooms and suites date from the late 1920s, and some of the 1930s furniture once graced the staterooms of the decommissioned *SS Normandie*.

⌧ **53-55 Brook St W1**
☎ **7629 8860; fax 7499 2210** e **info@claridges .co.uk; www.claridges .co.uk** ↔ **Bond Street** ✗ **Gordon Ramsay**

### Halkin (3, J2)

The 41-room Halkin is for travellers of a minimalist bent: lots of burlwood, marble and round glass things. Bedrooms are wood-panelled and stylishly uncluttered; staff paddle about in Armani uniforms.

⌧ **5 Halkin St SW1**
☎ **7333 1000; fax 7333 1100** e **res@ halkin.co.uk; www .halkin.co.uk** ↔ **Hyde Park Corner** ✗ **Nahm restaurant**

### One Aldwych (6, C8)

What was once an Art Nouveau newspaper office is now a 105-room hotel with modern art everywhere the eye rests and a merry, upbeat atmosphere. There's no sign outside, but the smell of money will lead you to the door.

⌧ **1 Aldwych WC2**
☎ **7300 1000; fax 7300 1001** e **reservations@ onealdwych.co.uk; www.onealdwych .co.uk** ↔ **Covent Garden, Charing Cross** ✗ **Axis & Indigo restaurants**

### The Ritz (6, E2)

What can we say about a hotel that has lent its name to the English lexicon? Arguably London's most celebrated hotel, the 130-room ritzy Ritz has a spectacular view over Green Park and is the royal family's 'home away from home'.

⌧ **150 Piccadilly W1**
☎ **7493 8181; fax 7493 2687** e **enquire@ theritzhotel.co.uk; www.theritzlondon.com** ↔ **Green Park** ✗ **Ritz restaurant, Palm Court (afternoon tea)**

### The Savoy (6, C8)

The landmark 228-room hotel is built on the site of the Savoy Palace, which was burned down during the Peasants' Revolt of 1381. Its rooms are so comfortable and have such great views that some people have been known to take up permanent residence here.

⌧ **Strand WC2**
☎ **7836 4343; fax 7240 6040** e **info@ the-savoy.co.uk; www.savoy-group .co.uk** ↔ **Charing Cross** ✗ **The Savoy Grill, The Thames Foyer (afternoon tea)**

*For luxurious Art Deco cab it to class-act Claridge's.*

Neil Setchfield

# TOP END

## Basil Street (3, J1)

This antique-stuffed 80-room hideaway in the heart of Knightsbridge is perfectly placed for carrying back the shopping from Harrods, Harvey Nichols or the boutiques of Sloane St.
✉ Basil St SW3
☎ 7581 3311; fax 7581 3693
e reservations@the-basil.com; www.the-basil.com ✆ Knightsbridge ✕ The Dining Room

## Blakes (2, J4)

For classic style, one of your first choices in London should be Blakes: five Victorian houses knocked into one hotel and decked out with four-poster beds, rich fabrics and antiques on stripped hardwood floorboards.
✉ 33 Roland Gardens SW7 ☎ 7370 6701; fax 7373 0442 e blakes@easynet.co.uk; www.blakeshotels.com ✆ South Kensington, Gloucester Road ✕ Blakes restaurant

## Charlotte Street (3, D5)

This wonderful 52-room hotel, where Laura Ashley goes postmodern and lives to tell the tale, has become a favourite of visiting media types.
✉ 15-17 Charlotte St W1 ☎ 7806 2000; fax 7806 2002 e charlotte@firmdale.com; www.charlottestreethotel.com ✆ Goodge Street ✕ Oscar restaurant

## Gore (2, G5)

This splendid 54-room hotel is a Victorian palace of polished mahogany, Turkish carpets, antique-style bathrooms, potted aspidistras and portraits and prints (some 4500 of them).
✉ 189 Queen's Gate SW7 ☎ 7584 6601; fax 7589 8127
e reservations@gorehotel.co.uk; www.gorehotel.co.uk ✆ High Street Kensington, Gloucester Road ✕ Bistrot 190 restaurant

## Great Eastern (3, D14)

A 19th-century Victorian pile above Liverpool Street train station has metamorphosed into a 267-room modernist palace, complete with a slew of Conran-inspired eating and drinking outlets.
✉ Liverpool St EC2 ☎ 7618 5000; fax 7618 5001 e reservations@great-eastern-hotel.co.uk; www.great-eastern-hotel.co.uk ✆ Liverpool Street ✕ Miyabi & Fishmarket restaurants, Terminus Bar & Grill

HAZLITT'S
BUILT
1718

Simon Bracken

## Hazlitt's (6, B5)

Built in 1718 from three Georgian houses, this is one of central London's finest hotels, with efficient personal service. All 23 rooms bear the names of former residents or visitors to the house and are individually decorated with antique furniture and prints.
✉ 6 Frith St, Soho Sq W1 ☎ 7434 1771; fax 7439 1524

e reservations@hazlitts.co.uk; www.hazlittshotel.com ✆ Tottenham Court Road

## Number Sixteen (2, H5)

Well situated on leafy Sumner Place, just off Brompton Rd, Number Sixteen is a smart, 35-room hotel with a cosy drawing room, library lounge and lovely garden.
✉ 16 Sumner Pl SW7 ☎ 7589 5232; fax 7584 8615 e sixteen@firmdale.com; www.numbersixteenhotel.co.uk ✆ South Kensington

## Portobello (2, F3)

This beautifully appointed 24-room place is in a great location and is one of the most attractive hotels in London. It has an exclusive feel to it; it's pricey but most people consider it money well spent.
✉ 22 Stanley Gardens W11 ☎ 7727 2777;

## Accommodation Guides

The London Tourist Board's (LTB) *Where to Stay & What to Do in London* (£4.99) lists approved hotels, guesthouses, apartments and B&Bs. It also publishes the free *Where to Stay on a Budget*. Useful Web sites include: e www.frontdesk.co.uk, e www.hotelsoflondon.co.uk and e www.londonlodging.co.uk.

fax 7792 9641 **e** info@
portobello-hotel.co.uk;
**www.portobello-hotel
.co.uk** ✆ Notting Hill
Gate

**Rookery** (3, C10)
This 33-room hotel has
been built within a row of
once-derelict 18th-century
Georgian houses. The
Rookery is fitted out with
period furniture (including
a museum-quality collec-
tion of Victorian bath-
room fixtures), original
Irish wood panelling and
open fires.
✉ Peter's La,
Cowcross St EC1
☎ 7336 0931;
fax 7336 0932
**e** reservations@
rookery.co.uk; www
.rookeryhotel.com
✆ Farringdon

*The homely Rookery*

# MID-RANGE

**Abbey House** (2, G4)
Just west of Kensington
Palace, Abbey House is a
particularly good-value small
hotel, with pretty Laura
Ashley-ish decor and very
high standards. Readers
seem to love this place.
✉ 11 Vicarage Gate
**W8** ☎ 7727 2594; fax
7727 1873 **e** www
.abbeyhousekensinton
.com ✆ High Street
Kensington

**Annandale House**
(2, H6) At the bend of a
quiet, tree-lined street, this dis-
crete and traditional hotel is
a good choice for the noise-
sensitive. All rooms have en-
suite facilities, phone and TV.
✉ 39 Sloane Gardens

SW1 ☎ 7730 5051; fax
7730 2727 ✆ Sloane
Square

**Crescent** (3, B6)
The Crescent Hotel is a
friendly, family-owned
operation in the heart of
Bloomsbury. Its 27 rooms
are maintained at a very
high standard.
✉ 49-50 Cartwright
Gardens WC1 ☎ 7387
1515; fax 7383 2054
**e** www.crescent
hoteloflondon.com
✆ Russell Square

**Edward Lear** (3, E1)
Once the home of the
eponymous Victorian painter
and poet (well, limerick
writer), the 31 rooms in this
small, comfortable place
have all the mod cons.
✉ 28-30 Seymour St W1
☎ 7402 5401; fax 7706
3766 **e** reception@ed
lear.com; www.edlear
.com ✆ Marble Arch

**Fielding** (6, B7)
In a pedestrian precinct a
block away from the Royal
Opera House, this small
hotel is remarkably good
value, clean and central.
The novelist Henry Fielding
(1707-54) lived nearby.
✉ 4 Broad Court, Bow
St WC2 ☎ 7836 8305;
fax 7497 0064
**e** reservations@
the-fielding-hotel
.co.uk; www.the-
fielding-hotel.co.uk
✆ Covent Garden

**Gate** (2, F3)
The bright and airy rooms
at the Gate, an old con-
verted town house with
classic frilly English decor
and lovely floral window
boxes, all have private
facilities.
✉ 6 Portobello Rd
W11 ☎ 7221 0707;
fax 7221 9128
**e** gatehotel@the
gate.globalnet.co.uk;
www.gatehotel.com
✆ Notting Hill Gate

## Serviced Apartments
Families or groups may prefer to rent a flat than stay in
a hotel or B&B. Several agencies can help track something down, including **Apartment Services London**
(☎ 7388 3558; fax 7383 7255; **e** aptserltd@
aol.com), **Aston's Budget & Designer Studios**
(☎ 7590 6000; fax 7590 6060; **e** sales@
astonsapartments.com, www.astonsapartments.com)
and **London Holiday Accommodation** (☎ 7485
0117; **e** sales@londonholiday.co.uk; www.london
holiday.co.uk).

### Hotel 167 (2, H4)

Hotel 167 is a small, stylish place and has unusually uncluttered and attractive decor. All 19 rooms have private bathrooms.

✉ 167 Old Brompton Rd SW5 ☎ 7373 0672; fax 7373 3360 e enquiries@hotel167 .com; www.hotel167 .com ⊖ Gloucester Road

### Inverness Court

(2, F4) This impressive pile was commissioned by Edward VII for his 'confidante', actress Lily Langtry, complete with a private theatre, now the cocktail bar. The panelled walls, stained glass and huge open fires of the public areas give it a Gothic feel but most of the 183 guestrooms – some overlooking Hyde Park – are modern.

✉ Inverness Terrace W2 ☎ 7229 1444; fax 7706 4240 e info@ cghotels.com; www .cghotels.com ⊖ Queensway

### La Gaffe (4, A1)

La Gaffe, above a popular Italian restaurant of the same name, is an eccentric but nonetheless comfortable hotel in an 18th-century cottage.

✉ 107-111 Heath St NW3 ☎ 7435 8965; fax 7794 7592 e la-gaffe@ msn.com,www.lagaffe .co.uk ⊖ Hampstead ✕ La Gaffe

### Pavilion (2, E5)

The Pavilion has 30 individually themed rooms ('Enter the Dragon' chinoiserie, 'Highland Fling' Scottish, 'Casablanca Nights' Moorish) to reflect its slogan/motto: 'Fashion, Glam & Rock 'n' Roll'. It's over the top but refreshingly different.

✉ 34-36 Sussex Gardens W2 ☎ 7262 0905; fax 7262 1324 e pavilionlondon@aol .com; www.msi.com .mt/pavilion/ ⊖ Paddington

### Philbeach (2, J3)

This fine budget to mid-range hotel is popular with gays and lesbians. It has a great garden restaurant and a fab basement bar.

✉ 30-31 Philbeach Gardens SW5 ☎ 7373 1244; fax 7244 0149 e philbeachhotel @freeserve.co.uk ⊖ Earl's Court ✕ Wilde About Oscar restaurant

### Swiss House (2, H4)

The Swiss House is a clean and welcoming 17-room hotel, a short distance from the heart of South Kensington, that has something of a country feel about it.

✉ 171 Old Brompton Rd SW5 ☎ 7373 2769; fax 7373 4983 e recep@swiss-hh .demon.co.uk; www .swiss-hh.demon.co.uk ⊖ Gloucester Road

£149

### Windermere (2, H7)

The 22 small but individually designed rooms (eight of them nonsmoking) are in a sparkling white Victorian town house with its own restaurant.

✉ 142-144 Warwick Way SW1 ☎ 7834 5163; fax 7630 8831 e windermere@ compuserve.com; www.windermere-hotel.co.uk ⊖ Victoria ✕ Pimlico Room

## BUDGET  Bob 90

### Alhambra (3, A7)

A great find in this area and handy for the station, this 52-room hotel is a simple but spotlessly clean place run by a charming family for over 20 years.

✉ 17-19 Argyle St WC1 ☎ 7837 9575; fax 7916 2476 e post master@alhambra hotel.com; www .alhambrahotel.com ⊖ King's Cross St Pancras

### Balmoral House

(2, F5) This immaculate and very comfortable hotel, with two properties directly opposite one another, is one of the better places to stay along Sussex Gardens.

✉ 156 & 157 Sussex Gardens W2 ☎ 7723 7445; fax 7402 0118 e info@balmoral househotel.co.uk ⊖ Paddington

### Celtic (3, C7)

The Celtic and its more expensive sister hotel, **St Margaret's** (26 Bedford Place WC1; 3, C7; ☎ 7636 4277; fax 7323 3066), are exceedingly friendly, clean and in the heart of Bloomsbury.

✉ 61-63 Guilford St WC1 ☎ 7837 9258; fax 7837 6737 ⊖ Russell Square

*Base2Stay Kensington*
*malMaison*

### County Hall (3, H8)

This Travel Inn in the former London County Hall, offers a one-price, one-room deal (£74.95 for up to two adults and two children). Its 150 rooms are fairly spartan but it's next to London's IMAX Cinema and the gigantic BA London Eye Ferris wheel. The **Euston Travel Inn Capital** (1 Dukes Rd WC1; 3, B6; ☎ 7554 3400, fax 7554 3419) offers the same deal. ✉ **Belvedere Rd SE1** ☎ 7902 1600; fax 7902 1619 e www .travelinn.co.uk ⊖ **Westminster**

*08702383300*

### Europa House (2, F5)

Europa House is another excellent choice on Sussex Gardens and you're always assured a warm welcome. The best of its 18 rooms are in the back. ✉ **151 Sussex Gardens W2** ☎ 7723 7343; fax 7224 9331 e europa house@enterprise.net; www.europahouse hotel.com ⊖ **Paddington**

### Garden Court (2, F4)

One of Bayswater's best options and just barely in this category, the Garden Court is a well-run and -maintained family hotel cobbled from two town houses (1870), and all its 34 rooms have phone and TV. Readers have raved about it. ✉ **30-31 Kensington Gardens Sq W2** ☎ 7229 2553; fax 7727 2749 e info@garden courthotel.co.uk; www .gardencourthotel.co.uk ⊖ **Bayswater**

### Luna Simone (5, G6)

If all London's budget hotels were like the spotlessly clean and comfortable 35-room Luna-Simone, we would all be happy campers. A full English breakfast and free bag-storage facilities are included in the price. ✉ **47 Belgrave Rd SW1** ☎ 7834 5897; fax 7828 2474 e lunasimone@ talk21.com; www .lunasimonehotel.com ⊖ **Victoria**

### Manzi's (6, C5)

This basic place, above a seafood restaurant just north of Leicester Square, is central and atmospheric; Johann Sebastian Strauss stayed here in 1838 when it was the Hôtel de Commerce. ✉ **1-2 Leicester St WC2** ☎ 7734 0224; fax 7437 4864 ⊖ **Leicester Square** ✗ Manzi's restaurant

### Portobello Gold

(2, F3) This somewhat louche hotel has a pleasant restaurant and bar on the ground floor and an Internet cafe upstairs that guests can use for free. ✉ **95-97 Portobello Rd W11** ☎ 7460 4913; fax 7229 2278 e www .portobellogold.com ⊖ **Notting Hill Gate** ✗ Portobello Gold restaurant

### St David's (2, E5)

Right in the centre of the action, the 74-room St David's Hotel is clean and comfortable with the usual out-of-control decor. Count on a warm reception. ✉ **14-20 Norfolk Sq W2** ☎ 7723 3856; fax 7402 9061 e info@ stdavidshotels.com; www.stdavidshotels .com ⊖ **Paddington**

### York House (2, J3)

York House is good value for what and where it is – on a quiet crescent – and the welcome is warm. The 27 rooms are basic, though; only a handful have showers. ✉ **27-28 Philbeach Gardens SW5** ☎ 7373 7519; fax 7370 4641 e yorkhh@aol.com ⊖ **Earl's Court**

## Hostels

Given the high cost of accommodation (and almost everything else) in London, travellers on a budget might consider staying at some of London's better independent hostels, where there are no age restrictions, and singles/doubles (from £36/48) are available along with dormitory accommodation. Two of the better ones are: **Ashlee House**, 261-265 Gray's Inn Rd WC1 (3, A7; ☎ 7833 9400; fax 7833 9677; e info@ash leehouse.co.uk,www.ashleehouse.co.uk; ⊖ King's Cross St Pancras) and **Generator**, Compton Place, 37 Tavistock Place WC1 (3, B7; ☎ 7388 7655; fax 7388 7644; e info@the-generator.co.uk, www.the-gener ator.co.uk; ⊖ Russell Square).

Neil Setchfield

# facts for the visitor

Simon Bracken

*Flying into Stansted? Your best bet is to take a train to London's Liverpool Street station.*

# ARRIVAL & DEPARTURE

London can be reached by air from virtually anywhere in the world and by bus, train and boat from continental Europe and Ireland. There are nonstop connections from the USA, Australasia and most European cities.

## Air

London has five main airports: Heathrow, the largest, followed by Gatwick, Stansted, London City and Luton. Most major airlines have ticket offices in London – consult the 'Airlines' entry in the *Yellow Pages* for addresses and phone numbers.

## Heathrow

Some 15 miles (24km) west of central London, Heathrow (1, B4; LHR; ☎ 0870 000 0123; e www.baa.co.uk/heathrow) is the world's busiest commercial airport; it has four terminals, with another on the way. Each terminal has competitive currency-exchange facilities, information counters and accommodation desks.

The vast majority of flight traffic is through Terminals 1, 2 and 3. Airlines using Terminal 4 include: Air Malta; British Airways (BA) intercontinental flights excluding Miami; BA European flights to Amsterdam, Athens, Basle, Moscow and Paris; Emirates Abu Dhabi flights operated by BA; KLM Royal Dutch Airlines; Kenya Airways; Qantas Airways; Sri Lankan Airlines.

### Left Luggage

There are left-luggage facilities (£3.50/4 for 12/24hrs) at: Terminal 1 (☎ 8745 5301; 5am-11pm), Terminal 2 (☎ 8745 4599; 5.30am-10.30pm); Terminal 3 (☎ 8759 3344; 24hrs); and Terminal 4

(☎ 8745 7460; 5am-11pm). All can forward baggage.

### Airport Access

**Train** The fastest way to get to central London is via the Heathrow Express (☎ 0845 600 1515; e www.heathrowexpress.co.uk; £12/23 single/return, children free; 15mins; every 15mins 5.00am-11.50pm) linking Heathrow Central (serving Terminals 1-3) and Terminal 4 stations with Paddington station (2, E5).

**Underground** The cheapest way to get to Heathrow from central London is via London Underground's Piccadilly Line (£3.60; 1hr; every 5-10mins 5.30am-11.45pm). There are two tube stations, one serving Terminals 1, 2 and 3, the other serving Terminal 4. There are ticket machines in the baggage-reclaim areas of all terminals.

**Bus** Airbus A2 (☎ 08075 747777; e www.gobycoach.com; £7/10 single/return; 1¾hrs; every 30mins) links King's Cross station with all Heathrow terminals, via Baker Street tube station, Marble Arch and Notting Hill Gate. The Hotel Hoppa bus (☎ 08705 747777; £2.50; every 10-30mins 5.30am-11.30pm) runs to 15 international hotels near the airport.

**Taxi** A black cab to/from central London costs about £40.

## Gatwick

Smaller, better-organised Gatwick (1, D4; LGW; ☎ 0870 000 2468; e www.baa.co.uk/gatwick) is 30 miles (48km) south of central London. The North and South Terminals are linked by an efficient monorail service; journey time between the two is about 2mins.

## Left Luggage
The left-luggage office at the North Terminal (☎ 01293-502013) opens 6am-10pm; the South Terminal office (☎ 01293-502014) operates 24hrs. They charge £3.50/4 for 6/24hrs.

## Airport Access
**Train** The Gatwick Express (☎ 0870 530 1530; [e] www.gatwickexpress .co.uk; £10.50/20 single/return; 30mins; every 15mins 5.20am-12.50am, then hourly) links the South Terminal station with Victoria.

The Connex South Central service (☎ 0845 748 4950; [e] www.connex .co.uk; £8.20; every 15-30mins, hourly in the wee hours) to/from Victoria is slower but cheaper.

There's also a Thameslink service (☎ 0845 748 4950; [e] www .thameslink.co.uk; from £9.80) to/from King's Cross, Farringdon and London Bridge.

**Bus** Airbus No 5 (☎ 08075 747 777; [e] www.gobycoach.com; £8.50/10 single/return; 16/day) operates 6am-11pm from Victoria Coach Station to Gatwick (to London: 4.15am-9.15pm).

**Taxi** A black cab to/from central London costs around £70.

## Stansted
At 35 miles (56km) to the north-east of central London, Stansted (STN; ☎ 0870 000 0303; [e] www.baa .co.uk/stansted) is London's third-busiest international gateway and its most attractive. The futuristic terminal building was designed by Norman Foster.

## Airport Access
**Train** The Stansted Express (☎ 0845 748 4950; [e] www.stanstedexpress .com; £13/21 single/return; 45mins; every 30mins) goes direct to Liverpool St station (3, D14) 6am-midnight (to airport: 5am-11pm).

**Bus** Airbus A6 (☎ 08075 747777; [e] www.gobycoach.com; £7/10 single/return) links Stansted with Victoria Coach Station every 30mins 3.30am-11.30pm, then hourly (to airport: every 30mins 4.05am-11.35pm, then hourly).

**Taxi** A black cab to/from central London costs about £70-80.

## London City
London City Airport (LCY; ☎ 7646 0000; [e] www.londoncityairport .com), 6 miles (10km) east of central London in the Docklands, has flights to 20 continental European cities as well as eight national destinations.

## Airport Access
**Bus** The blue airport Shuttlebus (☎ 7646 0088; [e] www.london cityairport.com/shuttlebus) connects London City with Liverpool Street station (£6/12 single/return; 25mins) and Canary Wharf (£3/6; 10mins) every 10-15mins 6.50am-10pm.

The green airport Shuttlebus (☎ 7646 0088; [c] www.londoncity airport.com/shuttlebus; £2/4 single/return; 5mins; every 10mins 6am-10.20pm) links London City and Canning Town station, which is on the Jubilee tube, Docklands Light Railway (DLR) and Silverlink/North London lines.

**Taxi** A black cab to/from central London costs about £20.

## Luton
A small, remote airport some 35 miles (56km) to the north of central London, Luton (LTN; ☎ 01582-405100; [e] www.londonluton.co .uk) caters mainly for cheap charter flights, though the discount airline easyJet (☎ 0870 600 0000; [e] www .easyjet.com) operates scheduled services from here.

## Airport Access

**Train** Thameslink (☎ 0845 748 4950; e www.thameslink.co.uk; £9.50; 30-40mins; every 15mins 7am-10pm) runs trains from King's Cross and other central London stations to Luton Airport Parkway station, from where an airport shuttle bus will take you to the airport (8mins).

**Bus** Green Line bus No 757 (☎ 0870 608 7261; e www.greenline.co.uk; £8/13 single/return; 1½hrs) serves Luton, from Buckingham Palace Rd south of Victoria train station, every 30mins 8am-8pm, then hourly (to airport: every 30mins 7.05am-10pm, then hourly).

**Taxi** A black cab to/from central London costs £70-80.

## Bus

### Within the UK

Bus travellers to/from London arrive at/depart from Victoria Coach Station (164 Buckingham Palace Rd SW1; 2, H7; ☎ 7730 3466). Queues can be horrendous, so try to book over the phone (☎ 7730 3499; Mon-Sat 9am-7pm). National Express (☎ 0870 580 8080; e www.goby coach.com) runs the largest bus network and is a member company of Eurolines. There are smaller competitors on the main UK routes, such as Green Line (☎ 0870 608 7261; e www.greenline.co.uk), an umbrella group of bus companies.

### Continental Europe

You can still get to/from continental Europe by bus without using the Channel Tunnel. You can book Eurolines tickets direct (52 Grosvenor Gardens SW1; ☎ 0870 514 3219; e www.eurolines.com) or through National Express, at Victoria Coach Station, or via travel agents.

## Train

### Within the UK

The main national rail routes are served by InterCity trains, which travel up to 140 miles/hr (225km/h). Same-day returns and one-week advance purchase are the cheapest tickets for those not holding rail passes, a wide variety of which are available from all main-line train stations. National Rail Enquiries (☎ 0845 748 4950) has timetables, fare and booking-number information. Check timetables and frequencies at e www.rail.co.uk/ukrail.

### Continental Europe

For European train enquiries contact Rail Europe (☎ 0870 584 8848; e www.eurostarplus.com).

**Eurostar** Travelling via the Channel Tunnel, the high-speed passenger rail service Eurostar (☎ 0870 518 6186, 01233-617575 from outside the UK; e www.eurostar .com) links London's Waterloo station (3, H9) with Paris' Gare du Nord (3hrs; up to 25/day) and Brussels (2hrs 40mins; up to 12/day); some trains also stop at Lille and Calais in France and Ashford in England. Fares vary enormously but a cheap APEX return from Paris/Brussels costs €150/108.

**Le Shuttle** Trains (☎ 0870 535 3535; e www.eurotunnel.com) transport motor vehicles and bicycles between Folkestone in England and Coquelles in France (3 miles/5km south-west of Calais); they run up to every 15mins (hourly 1am-6am). Five-day excursion fares (€120-320 for car and passengers from France) can be booked in advance or purchased at the tollgate. Same-day returns cost €99-267.

## Travel Documents

### Passport

Passports must be valid for six months from date of entry.

### Visa

Visas aren't required by nationals of Australia, Canada, New Zealand, South Africa and the USA for stays of up to six months; European Union (EU) citizens don't require a visa and can stay indefinitely. Others should check with their local UK diplomatic mission.

### Return/Onward Ticket

A return ticket may be required and you may have to prove that you have sufficient funds to support yourself; a credit card will help.

## Customs

Like all EU nations, the UK has a two-tier customs system: one for goods bought duty-free and one for goods bought in an EU country where taxes and duties have already been paid.

The limits for goods purchased duty-free *outside* the EU are: 200 cigarettes or 250g of tobacco; 2L of still wine plus 1L of spirits over 22% or another 2L wine (sparkling or still); 50g of perfume, 250cc of toilet water; other goods (including cider and beer) up to the value of £145.

You can buy items in another EU county, where certain goods might be cheaper, and bring them into the UK so long as duty and tax have been paid on them. Allowances are: 800 cigarettes; 200 cigars and 1kg of tobacco; 10L of spirits; 20L of fortified wines; 90L of wine (sparkling limited to 60L); and 110L of beer.

## Departure Tax

This is almost always built into the price of your ticket. It costs £10/20 for EU/other destinations.

# GETTING AROUND

Everybody complains about the London Underground – and with good reason – but it is still *the* way to travel in this enormous city. Buses can prove more pleasant, particularly for visitors, but traffic congestion has reduced their speed to a snail's crawl. Black cabs (ie, officially registered ones) are comfortable, efficient and expensive.

### Information

For general information about the Underground, buses, DLR or local trains call ☎ 7222 1234 or visit the Underground (**e** www.thetube.com) or Transport for London (**e** www .transportforlondon.gov.uk) Web sites. For news of how services are running, call Travelcheck (☎ 7222 1200).

## Travel Passes

One-day Travelcards usually offer the cheapest method of travelling, and can be used after 9.30am weekdays (anytime at weekends) on all forms of transport – tubes, main-line trains, the DLR and buses (including night buses). Most visitors find that a one-day Travelcard for Zones 1 and 2 (£4.10/2 adult/child) is sufficient. If you plan to start moving before 9.30am Mon-Fri, you can buy a Peak Travelcard for Zones 1 and 2 for £5.30/2.60.

Weekly Travelcards are available but require an ID card with a passport-sized photo. A card for Zones 1 and 2, allowing you to travel at any time of day, costs £19.30/7.90. A Weekend Travelcard valid weekends in Zones 1 and 2 costs £6.10/3. Family Travelcards, costing from £2.70/80p per adult/child for Zones 1 and 2, allow one or two adults and up to four children to travel together.

## Underground

The 12 lines of the Underground, or 'tube', extend as far afield as Buckinghamshire, Essex and Heathrow. It's a slow, unreliable, ageing and expensive system but normally the quickest and easiest way to get around. There are Underground travel information centres at all Heathrow terminals, a half-dozen major tube stations and at larger main-line train stations.

### Fares & Passes

The Underground is divided into six concentric zones. The basic fare for Zone 1 is £1.60/60p adult/child; to cross all six zones (eg, to/from Heathrow) it costs £3.60/1.50. A carnet of 10 tickets for Zone 1 costs £11.50/5. If you're travelling through a couple of zones or several times in one day, consider a travel pass good on all forms of transport (p. 111).

## Bus

If you're not in a hurry, travelling around on London's red double-decker buses can be more enjoyable than using the tube. The *Central London Bus Guide Map* and a number of individual area maps are free from most travel information centres or call ☎ 7371 0247 to have one sent. For general information on London buses call ☎ 7222 1234 (24hrs). For news on services call Travelcheck (☎ 7222 1200).

### Fares & Passes

Single-journey bus tickets sold on the bus cost £1 in central London and 70p elsewhere in London. Those aged five to 15 pay a uniform 40p. A one-day bus pass valid throughout London and before 9.30am costs £2/1 adult/child.

### Night Bus

Trafalgar Square (6, E6) is the focal point for most night buses (prefixed with the letter 'N'). They stop on request midnight-7am but services can be infrequent. Normal bus fares are charged; Travelcard-holders ride free.

### Useful Bus Routes

One of the best ways to explore London is to buy a Travelcard and jump on a bus (especially the double-decker Routemaster ones, with a conductor and an access platform at the rear that makes jumping on and off so easy). Some bus routes that are useful for visitors include Nos 8, 9, 10, 19 and 24.

### Accessible Bus Travel

Wheelchair-accessible Stationlink buses (☎ 7941 4600), with driver-operated ramps, follow a similar route to that of the Underground's Circle Line and join up all mainline stations. From Paddington, there are hourly services clockwise (route SL1) 8.15am-7.15pm and anticlockwise (SL2) 8.40am-6.40pm.

## DLR & Train

The driverless Docklands Light Railway (DLR) links the City at Bank and Tower Gateway at Tower Hill, with services to Stratford to the east and the Docklands and Greenwich to the south. The DLR runs weekdays 5.30am-12.30am (shorter hrs at weekends); fares are the same as for the tube. For general information on the DLR call ☎ 7363 9700 or visit e www.dlr.co.uk. For news of how the DLR and Docklands bus services are running, call the 24hr Docklands Travel Hotline on ☎ 7918 4000.

Several rail companies also operate passenger trains in London, including the Silverlink (or North London) line (☎ 01923 207258; e www.silverlinktrains.com), which links Richmond in the south-west and North Woolwich in the south-east, and the crowded Thameslink (☎ 0845 748 4950; e www.thameslink.co.uk) 'sardine line' that runs from Elephant & Castle and London Bridge in the south through the City to King's Cross and as far north as Luton. Most lines interchange with the tube and Travelcards can be used on both systems.

## Taxi

The 'black cab' is as much a feature of the London cityscape as the red double-decker bus. Cabs are available for hire when the yellow light above the windscreen is illuminated. Fares are metered, with flag fall at £1.40 and increments of 20p. To order a cab by phone try Radio Taxis on ☎ 7272 0272; they will also charge for the cost of getting to you, up to £3.80.

Minicabs, some of which are now licensed, are cheaper freelance competitors to the cabs, but they can only be hired by phone or from a minicab office (every neighbourhood and high street has one). Some drivers have a very limited idea of how to get around efficiently (and safely) – you, the foreigner, may find yourself being pressed to navigate. Minicabs can carry up to four people and don't have meters, so it's essential to get a quote before you start; bargain hard – most drivers will start at about 25% higher than the fare they're prepared to accept.

Small companies are based in particular areas. Try one of the large

24hr operators: ☎ 7387 8888, 7272 2222, 7272 3322 or 8888 4444.

## Car & Motorcycle

Avoid bringing a car into London. Traffic moves slowly, parking is expensive and drivers are extremely aggressive. Traffic wardens and wheel clampers operate with extreme efficiency and if your vehicle is towed away, you won't see any change from £100 to get it back.

### Road Rules

Vehicles travel on the left-hand side of the road; give way to your right at roundabouts. Wearing seat belts in the front seat is compulsory and if they are fitted in the back, they must be worn as well. Motorcyclists must wear helmets at all times.

The current speed limits are 30mph (48km/h) in built-up areas, 60mph (97km/h) on single carriageways, and 70mph (113km/h) on motorways and dual carriageways. A blood-alcohol level of 35mg/100mL is the current limit while driving.

### Rental

Car-hire rates are very pricey; the big international rental firms charge from £40 a day and £150-200 a week for their smallest cars (Ford Fiesta, Peugeot 106). The main firms include Avis (☎ 0870 606 0100; e www.avis.co.uk), Budget (☎ 0800 181181; e www.go-budget.com), Europcar (☎ 0870 607 5000; e www.europcar.co.uk), Hertz (☎ 0870 599 6699; e www.hertz.com) and Thrifty Car Rental (☎ 0800 731 1366, e www.thrifty.co.uk). Holiday Autos (☎ 0870 530 0400; e www.holidayautos.com) operates through several rental firms and usually offers great deals, starting at £135 a week.

### Driving Licence & Permits

Your normal driving licence is legal for 12 months after you enter the

UK, but it's also a good idea to carry an International Driving Permit (IDP), obtainable from your local motoring association for a small fee.

### Motoring Organisations

There are two principal motoring organisations within the UK. These are: the Automobile Association (AA; information ☎ 0800 028 8540, breakdown ☎ 0800 887766; e www.theaa.com) and the Royal Automobile Club (RAC; information ☎ 0800 550 550, breakdown ☎ 0800 828282; e www. rac.co.uk).

# PRACTICAL INFORMATION

## Climate & When to Go

London is a year-round destination. High season is June to August, with a better chance of good weather but also crowds and sold-out venues. In April/May or September/October the weather can still be good, and queues shorter. November to March are quieter. Expect cool weather and rain even in high summer.

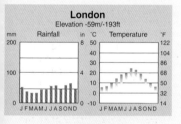

**London**
Elevation -59m/-193ft

## Tourist Information

### Tourist Information Abroad

The British Tourist Authority (BTA; ☎ 8846 9000; e www.visitbritain .com) stocks information on London with offices in the countries below:

Australia
  L16, The Gateway, 1 Macquarie Pl, Sydney NSW 2000 (☎ 02-9377 4400)

Canada
  Suite 120, 5915 Airport Rd, Mississauga, Ont L4V 1T1 (☎ 905-405 1840, toll-free ☎ 1-888 VISIT UK)

France
  Maison de la Grand Bretagne, 19 rue des Mathurins, 75009 Paris (☎ 01 44 51 56 20)

Ireland
  18-19 College Green, Dublin 2 (☎ 01-670 8000)

Netherlands
  Aurora Gebouw (5e) Stadhouderskade 2, 1054 ES Amsterdam (☎ 020-607 0002)

New Zealand
  17th flr, NZI House, 151 Queen St, Auckland 1 (☎ 09-303 1446)

South Africa
  Lancaster Gate, Hyde Park La, Hyde Park 2196 (☎ 011-325 0343)

USA
  Suite 701, 551 5th Ave, New York, NY 10176-0799 (☎ 212-986 2200, toll-free ☎ 1-800 GO 2 BRITAIN)
  Suite 570, 10880 Wiltshire Blvd, Los Angeles, CA 90024 (☎ 310-470 2782)

### Local Tourist Information

Both the Britain Visitor Centre run by the British Tourism Authority (BTA) and the London Tourist Board's (LTB) assorted tourist information centres handle walk-ins only. Otherwise, call the BTA (☎ 8846 9000; e www.visitbritain .com) or the LTB (☎ 7932 2000; e www.londontouristboard.com). The LTB also has the London Line (☎ 09068 663344; 60p), which can fill you in on everything from tourist attractions and events to river trips and tours, accommodation, theatre, shopping, eating, children's London and gay and lesbian venues.

**Britain Visitor Centre** The Britain Visitor Centre (1 Regent St SW1; 6, E4; ✆ Piccadilly Circus) has a tourist information, a hotel booking and travel desk, a shop with maps and books and a theatre-ticket agency (Mon 9.30am-6.30pm, Tues-Fri 9am-6.30pm, Sat-Sun 10am-4pm; Sat 9am-5pm June-Sept).

**Tourist Information Centres** The main TIC, on the forecourt of Victoria train station (5, G3) handles accommodation and travel bookings, and can arrange national coach and theatre tickets and opens Apr-Oct: Mon-Sat 8am-8pm, Sun 8am-6pm; Nov-Mar: Mon-Sat 8am-6pm, Sun 9am-4pm. Other TICs include: Arrivals Hall, Waterloo International Terminal (6, H8; 8.30am-10.30pm); Liverpool Street station (6, C14; 8am-6pm); Heathrow Terminals 1, 2 & 3 tube station 8am-6pm; all other airports have branches as do Paddington station and Victoria Coach Station.

The Corporation of London TIC (St Paul's Churchyard EC4; ✆ 7332 1456; e www.cityoflondon.gov.uk; ✆ St Paul's), opposite St Paul's Cathedral, opens Apr-Sept: 9.30am-5pm; Oct-Mar: Mon-Fri 9.30am-5pm, Sat 9.30am-12.30pm.

## Embassies & High Commissions

Australian High Commission
Australia House, Strand WC2 (3, E8; ✆ 7379 4334; e www.australia.org.uk; ✆ Temple/Holborn)

Canadian High Commission
Macdonald House, 1 Grosvenor Sq W1 (3, F3; ✆ 7258 6600; e www.canada.org.uk; ✆ Bond St)

French Consulate-General
6a Cromwell Pl SW7 (2, H5; ✆ 7838 2055; ✆ South Kensington)

Irish Embassy & Chancery
*Embassy:* 17 Grosvenor Pl SW1 (3, J2; ✆ 7235 2171; ✆ Hyde Park Corner)
*Chancery:* Montpelier House, 106 Brompton Rd SW3 (✆ 7255 7700; ✆ South Kensington)

Royal Netherlands Embassy
38 Hyde Park Gate SW7 (2, G4; ✆ 7590 3200; ✆ High St Kensington)

New Zealand High Commission
New Zealand House, 80 Haymarket SW1 (6, E5; ✆ 7930 8422; e www.newzealandhc.uk; ✆ Piccadilly Circus)

South African High Commission
South Africa House, Trafalgar Sq WC2 (6, D6; ✆ 7451 7299; e www.southafricahouse.com; ✆ Trafalgar Square)

US Embassy
5 Upper Grosvenor St W1 (3, F2; ✆ 7499 9000; e www.usembassy.org.uk; ✆ Bond St)

## Money

### Currency
Unlike the majority of EU members, whose single currency is now the euro (€), Britain has retained its own monetary system – the pound sterling – and will continue to do so for the foreseeable future. The pound (£) is divided into 100 pence (p). Coins of 1p and 2p are copper; 5p, 10p, 20p and 50p are silver; the heavy £1 coin is a brassy gold; and the £2 coin is gold-coloured on the edge with a silver centre. Notes (bills) come in £5, £10, £20 and £50 denominations.

### Travellers Cheques
Thomas Cook (✆ 01733-318950) and American Express (Amex; ✆ 01222-666111) are widely accepted, don't charge for cashing their own cheques (though their exchange rates are not always competitive) and can often arrange replacements for lost or stolen cheques within 24hrs. Both have offices all over London.

## Credit Cards

The following cards are widely accepted in London. For cancellations, call:

| | |
|---|---|
| Amex | ☎ 01273-689955 or 696933 |
| Diners Club | ☎ 0800 460800 or 01252-516261 |
| JCB | ☎ 7499 3000 |
| MasterCard | ☎ 0800 964767 |
| Visa | ☎ 0800 895082 |

## ATMs

You'll find Automatic Teller Machines (ATMs) linked up to international money systems outside banks, at train stations and inside some pubs and retail outlets.

## Changing Money

Changing money is never a problem in London, with banks, bureaux de change and travel agencies all competing for business. There are 24hr exchange bureaux at Heathrow Terminals 1, 3 and 4 (Terminal 2 bureau opens 6am-11pm).

The main Amex office (30-31 Haymarket; 6, D5; ☎ 7484 9610; ⊖ Piccadilly Circus) opens Mon-Fri 8.30am-7pm, Sat 9am-5.30pm and Sun 10am-4pm (an hour later at weekends in summer). Thomas Cook's main office (30 St James's St; 6, E3; ☎ 7853 6400; ⊖ Green Park) opens Mon-Fri 9am-5.30pm (Wed from 10am) and Sat 10am-4pm.

London banks are usually open Mon-Fri 9.30am-3.30pm, with some open Sat 9.30am-noon.

## Tipping

| | |
|---|---|
| Restaurants | 10-15% (usually inc.) |
| Taxis | round up to nearest £ |
| Porters | £2 per bag |

## Discounts

Most attractions offer discounts to children (check each venue for age limits), youth card-holders under 25 (or 26), students with ISIC cards (age limits may apply), over 60s (or 65; sometimes lower for women), disabled visitors and families.

## London Pass

The London Pass (☎ 0870 242 9988, e www.londonpass.com) allows free admission to over 50 museums and other attractions (see individual listings for details), and unlimited travel on the tube (Zones 1-6), buses and trains within central London. The pass costs £22/39/49/79 for 1/2/3/6 days (£14/24/30/42 for those aged 5-15).

## Student, Youth & Teachers' Cards

The International Student Identity Card (ISIC), the International Youth Travel Card (IYTC) issued by the Federation of International Youth Travel Organisations (FIYTO) and the International Teacher Identity Card (ITIC) can produce discounts on many forms of transport, admission to venues and meals in some university restaurants. All cards cost £6.

## Seniors' Cards

Many attractions offer reduced price admission for those aged over 60 or 65 (can be as low as 55 for women); ask even if you can't see a discount listed. The railways offer a Senior Citizen Railcard (£18) for those aged over 60.

## Travel Insurance

A policy covering theft, loss, medical expenses and compensation for cancellation or delays in your travel arrangements is highly recommended. If items are lost or stolen, make sure you get a police report straight away – otherwise your insurer will not pay up.

## Opening Hours

**Offices**
Mon-Fri 9am-5/5.30pm

**Shops**
Mon-Sat 9/10am-6pm (some open Sun 10am-4pm or 12-6pm)

**Late-Night Shopping**
Thurs 9/10am-8pm in the West End

## Public Holidays

Most banks and businesses are closed on public (or bank) holidays. Museums and other attractions may close on Christmas and Boxing days but usually stay open for other holidays. Some smaller museums close Monday and/or Tuesday, and some venues close Sunday morning.

| | |
|---|---|
| 1 Jan | New Year's Day |
| Late Mar/Apr | Good Friday |
| Late Mar/Apr | Easter Monday |
| May (1st Mon) | May Day Bank Holiday |
| May (last Mon) | Spring Bank Holiday |
| Aug (last Mon) | Summer Bank Holiday |
| 25 Dec | Christmas Day |
| 26 Dec | Boxing Day |

## Time

Wherever you are in the world, the time on your watch is measured in relation to Greenwich Mean Time (GMT), the time in London. British Summer Time (late March to late October) confuses things so that even London is 1hr ahead of GMT. At noon in London, in summer it's:

6am in New York
3am in Los Angeles
1pm in Paris
1pm in Johannesburg
11pm in Auckland
10pm in Sydney

## Electricity

The standard voltage throughout Britain is 230/240V AC, 50 Hz. Plugs have three square pins, but adapters to fit European-style plugs are widely available.

## Weights & Measures

The UK has now legally switched to the metric system though imperial equivalents are likely to be used for much of the population for some time to come. Distances continue to be given in miles, yards, feet and inches though most liquids – apart from milk and beer (which come in half-pints and pints) – are now sold in litres. See the conversion table on p. 122.

## Post

The Royal Mail, Britain's national postal service, is arguably the most efficient in the world, with 90% of letters bearing a 1st-class stamp posted before noon delivered the following morning *anywhere* in the country. Stamps are sold at post-office counters, vending machines outside post offices and at selected newsagents and corner shops.

For general postal enquiries call ☎ 0845 722 3344 or visit e www.royalmail.co.uk.

### Postal Rates
Domestic 1st-/2nd-class mail (up to 60g) costs 19/27p; postcards to Europe/Australasia and the Americas cost 36/65p.

### Opening Hours
London post offices usually open Mon-Fri 8.30/9am-5/5.30pm, with some main ones open Sat 9am-12/1pm. Trafalgar Square Post Office (GPO/poste restante) opens Mon-Fri 8.30am-6.30pm and Sat 9am-5.30pm.

## Telephone

Public phones, which are ubiquitous in London, are either coin-operated (min: 20p) or accept phonecards or credit cards.

## Phonecards

There's a wide range of local and international phonecards available at newsagents, including British Telecom (BT) phonecards available in £3, £5, £10 and £20 denominations. Lonely Planet's eKno Communication Card, specifically aimed at travellers, provides competitive international calls (avoid using it for local calls), messaging services and free email. Visit **e** www.ekno. lonelyplanet.com for information on joining and accessing the service.

## Mobile Phones

The UK uses the GSM 900 network, which covers continental Europe, Australia and New Zealand, but is not compatible with the North American GSM 1900 or the totally different system in Japan (some North Americans have GSM 1900/900 phones that do work here). Beware of local calls being routed internationally, which can be very expensive. You can also rent one (from about £20 per week) from various companies, including Mobell (☎ 0800 243524, **e** www.mobell.com) and Cellhire (☎ 08705 610610, **e** www.cell hire.com).

## Country & City Codes

| | |
|---|---|
| UK | ☎ 44 |
| London | ☎ 020 |

## Useful Numbers

| | |
|---|---|
| Directory Enquiries | ☎ 192 |
| International Dialling Code | ☎ 00 |
| International Directory Enquiries | ☎ 153 |
| Local & National Operator | ☎ 100 |
| Reverse-Charge/Collect Calls | ☎ 155 |
| Time | ☎ 123 |
| Weathercall (Greater London) | ☎ 0906 850 0401 |

## International Codes

| | |
|---|---|
| Australia | ☎ 0061 |
| Canada | ☎ 001 |
| Japan | ☎ 0081 |
| New Zealand | ☎ 0064 |
| South Africa | ☎ 0027 |
| USA | ☎ 001 |

# Email/www

Most hotels, hostels and even some pubs in London are geared up for Internet access.

## Internet Cafes

If you can't access the Internet from where you're staying, London is chock-a-block with cybercafes.

Cyberia
39 Whitfield St W1 (3, D5; ☎ 7681 4223; **e** www.cyberiacafe.net; 50p/5mins; open Mon-Fri 9am-8pm, Sat & Sun 11am-7pm)

easyEverything
12-14 Wilton Rd SW1 (3, K4; ☎ 7233 8456; **e** www.easyeverything.com; £1/10mins-1hr, depending on the time of day; open 24hrs)

Buzz Bar
95 Portobello Rd W11 (2, F3; ☎ 7460 4906; **e** www.buzzbar.co.uk; £1.50/30mins; open Mon-Sat 10am-7pm)

Webshack
15 Dean St W1 (6, B4; ☎ 7439 8000; **e** www.webshack-cafe.com; £2/hr, £1.25 after 8pm; open Mon-Sat 10am-11pm, Sun 1pm-9pm)

## Useful Sites

The Lonely Planet Web site (**e** www .lonelyplanet.com) offers a speedy link to many of London's Web sites. Others to try include:

Evening Standard
**e** www.thisislondon.com

London on Line
**e** www.londononline.co.uk

Time Out
**e** www.timeout.co.uk

UK Directory
**e** www.ukdirectory.com/travel

UK Weather
**e** www.meteo.gov.uk

## CitySync

CitySync *London*, Lonely Planet's digital guide for Palm OS hand-held devices, allows quick searches, sorting and bookmarking of hundreds of London's attractions, clubs, hotels, restaurants and more – all pinpointed on scrollable street maps. Purchase or demo CitySync *London* at **e** www.citysync.com.

# Doing Business

For word processing or other secretarial services go to Typing Overload (1st fl, 67 Chancery La WC2; 6, A10; ☎ 7404 5464; **e** www.typingoverload.com; ⊖ Chancery Lane). For photocopying, computer services such as scanning, computer rentals and video-conferencing, try Kinko's (328 High Holborn WC1; 3, D9; ☎ 7539 2900; **e** www.kinkos.com; ⊖ Chancery Lane).

The main sources of information are the *Financial Times* (Mon-Sat) and the weekly *Economist*. Government bodies and business associations that may be useful include the Confederation of British Industry (Centre Point, 103 New Oxford St, London WC1A 1DU; 6, A5; ☎ 7395 8195; **e** www.cbi.org.uk; ⊖ Tottenham Court Rd); Department of Trade & Industry (1 Victoria St, London SW1H 0ET; ☎ 7215 5000; **e** www.dti.gov.uk; ⊖ St James's Park); London Chamber of Commerce & Industry (33 Queen St, London EC4R 1AP; 3, F12; ☎ 7248 4444; **e** www.londonchamber.co.uk; ⊖ Mansion House); and Trade Partners UK (Department of Trade & Industry, Kingsgate House, 66-74 Victoria St, London SW1E 6SW; 3, J6; ☎ 7215 5444; **e** www.trade partners.gov.uk; ⊖ Victoria).

# Newspapers & Magazines

Most major newspapers in the UK are national; the only daily that is well and truly a Londoner is the *Evening Standard*, an afternoon tabloid. The bottom end of the newspaper market in terms of content – though tops in circulation – is occupied by the *Sun*, *Mirror*, *Daily Star* and *Daily Record* tabloids. The middle-level tabs, the *Daily Mail* and *Daily Express*, are very Conservative bastions. The *Telegraph* far outsells its other broadsheet rivals. *The Times* is conservative and influential. Others include the duller-than-dull *Independent* and the mildly left-wing *Guardian*. Almost every daily newspaper has a Sunday stablemate. See p. 84 for listings magazines.

# Radio

London's own radio stations include Capital FM (95.8FM), the favoured pop station in the city, and Capital Gold (1548AM) which plays 60s-80s oldies. BBC London Live (94.9FM) is a talk-back station with a London bias. Xfm (104.9FM) bills itself as an alternative radio station and plays indie music.

Among the national stations are:

BBC Radio 1 (98.8FM) – pop/rock/dance
BBC Radio 2 (89.1FM) – 60s, 70s and 80s goldies
BBC Radio 3 (91.3FM) – classical music and plays
BBC Radio 4 (93.5FM) – news, drama, talk
Radio 5 Live (909AM) – sport and news
BBC World Service (648AM) – coverage from around the world
Jazz FM (102.2FM) – jazz and blues
Classic FM (100.9FM) – classical music with commercials

# TV

Choose from BBC1 and BBC2 (publicly funded, without commercials); ITV, Channel 4 and Channel 5 (commercial); plus satellite and assorted cable channels.

## Photography & Video

Print film is widely available, but slide film can be harder to find; try any branch of Jessops including the one at 63-69 New Oxford St WC1 (6, A6; ☎ 7240 6077; ✆ Tottenham Court Rd).

The UK, like most of Europe and Australia, uses the PAL system, which is incompatible with the American and Japanese NTSC system.

## Health

### Immunisations

No jabs are needed to visit Britain.

### Precautions

Tap water is always safe. Whether you eat British beef or lamb after the bovine spongiform encephalopathy (BSE or 'mad cow disease') scare and the foot-and-mouth epidemic is up to you, but most carnivorous Londoners still do.

### Insurance & Medical Treatment

EU nationals and some others (including Australians and New Zealanders) can obtain free emergency medical treatment and subsidised dental care through the National Health Service (NHS). However, travel insurance is advisable to cover other expenses (eg, ambulance and repatriation).

### Medical Services

Hospitals with 24hr accident and emergency units include:

Guy's Hospital
  St Thomas St SE1 (3, H13; ☎ 7955 5000; ✆ London Bridge)

Royal Free Hospital
  Pond St NW3 (2, A5; ☎ 7794 0500; ✆ Belsize Park)

University College Hospital
  Grafton Way WC1 (3, C5; ☎ 7387 9300; ✆ Euston Square)

### Dental Services

To find an emergency dentist phone the Dental Emergency Care Service (☎ 7955 2186) Mon-Fri 8.45am-3.30pm or call into Eastman Dental Hospital (256 Gray's Inn Rd WC1; 3, B8; ☎ 7915 1000; ✆ King's Cross).

### Pharmacies

Chemists can advise on minor ailments. There is always one local chemist that opens 24hrs (see local newspapers or notices in chemist windows). Boots (75 Queensway W1; 2, F4; ☎ 7229 9266; ✆ Queensway or Bayswater) opens Mon-Sat 9am-10pm and Sun 5-10pm.

## Toilets

Toilets at main train stations, bus terminals and attractions are generally OK, usually with facilities for disabled people and those with young children. At the stations you usually have to pay 20p to use the facilities. Many disabled toilets require a special key. Ask at tourist offices or send a cheque or postal order for £3 to RADAR (see p. 121).

## Safety Concerns

London is remarkably safe considering its size and the disparity in wealth. That said, be careful at night and take particular care in crowded places such as the tube, where pickpockets and bag snatchers operate.

### Lost Property

Most items found on buses and tubes end up at Transport for London's Lost Property Office (200 Baker St NW1 5RZ; 3, C1; ✆ Baker St), open Mon-Fri 9.30am-2pm. Items left on main-line trains end up back at the main terminals; call ☎ 7928 5151 for the correct telephone number. For items left in black cabs, call ☎ 7918 2000.

## Keeping Copies

Make photocopies of all your important documents, keep some with you, separate from the originals, and leave a copy at home. You can also store details of documents in Lonely Planet's free online Travel Vault (e www.ekno.lonelyplanet .com), password-protected and accessible worldwide.

## Emergency Numbers

Ambulance, Fire & Police ☎ 999

## Women Travellers

Aside from the very occasional wolf-whistle and unwelcome body contact on the tube, women will find male Londoners reasonably enlightened.

### Information & Organisations

The Well Women Centre (Marie Stopes House, 108 Whitfield St W1; 3, C4; ☎ 0845 300 8090; ⊖ Warren St) dispenses advice on contraception and pregnancy Mon-Sat 9am-5pm (Tues & Wed to 8pm). The Rape & Sexual Abuse Helpline (☎ 8239 1122) operates Mon-Fri 12-2.30pm & 7pm-9.30pm, Sat & Sun 2.30pm-5pm.

## Gay & Lesbian Travellers

In general, Britain is fairly tolerant of homosexuality and London has a flourishing gay scene. But there remain pockets of out-and-out hostility, and overt displays of affection are not necessarily wise away from acknowledged gay venues and areas such as Old Compton St in Soho. The age of consent was recently lowered to 16 to bring it in line with that for heterosexuals.

### Information & Organisations

The 24hr Lesbian & Gay Switchboard (☎ 7837 7324) can help with most enquiries. London Friend (☎ 7837 3337) offers similar assistance 7.30pm-10pm. For listings magazines, see p. 99.

## Disabled Travellers

Large, new hotels and modern tourist venues are often accessible, unlike most older buildings. Newer buses and trains sometimes have steps that lower for easier access; check with Transport for London's Unit for Disabled Passengers (172 Buckingham Palace Rd SW1 9TN; ☎ 7918 3312). They publish the free *Access to the Underground*, which indicates which tube stations have ramps and lifts (all DLR stations do).

### Information & Organisations

The LTB has accessibility information for the disabled on its Web site (e www.londontouristboard .com). Information on wheelchair access to cultural venues in London is available from Artsline (☎ 7388 2227). The Royal Association for Disability and Rehabilitation (RADAR; Unit 12, City Forum, 250 City Rd, London EC1V 8AF; ☎ 7250 3222; e www .radar.org.uk) is an umbrella organisation for voluntary groups for the disabled and a useful source of information.

## Language

The English language is by far and away England's greatest contribution to the modern world, and London is its epicentre. These days, however, you'll encounter a veritable Babel of languages being spoken in London, and there are pockets of the capital where English is very much in the minority.

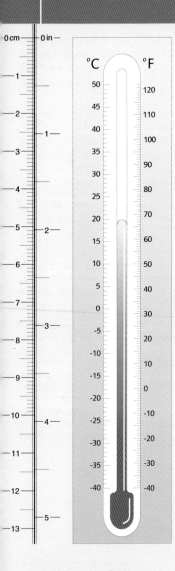

## Conversion Table

### Clothing Sizes
*Measurements approximate only; try before you buy.*

#### Women's Clothing

| Aust/NZ | 8 | 10 | 12 | 14 | 16 | 18 |
|---|---|---|---|---|---|---|
| Europe | 36 | 38 | 40 | 42 | 44 | 46 |
| Japan | 5 | 7 | 9 | 11 | 13 | 15 |
| UK | 8 | 10 | 12 | 14 | 16 | 18 |
| USA | 6 | 8 | 10 | 12 | 14 | 16 |

#### Women's Shoes

| Aust/NZ | 5 | 6 | 7 | 8 | 9 | 10 |
|---|---|---|---|---|---|---|
| Europe | 35 | 36 | 37 | 38 | 39 | 40 |
| France only | 35 | 36 | 38 | 39 | 40 | 42 |
| Japan | 22 | 23 | 24 | 25 | 26 | 27 |
| UK | 3½ | 4½ | 5½ | 6½ | 7½ | 8½ |
| USA | 5 | 6 | 7 | 8 | 9 | 10 |

#### Men's Clothing

| Aust/NZ | 92 | 96 | 100 | 104 | 108 | 112 |
|---|---|---|---|---|---|---|
| Europe | 46 | 48 | 50 | 52 | 54 | 56 |
| Japan | S | | M | M | | L |
| UK | 35 | 36 | 37 | 38 | 39 | 40 |
| USA | 35 | 36 | 37 | 38 | 39 | 40 |

#### Men's Shirts (Collar Sizes)

| Aust/NZ | 38 | 39 | 40 | 41 | 42 | 43 |
|---|---|---|---|---|---|---|
| Europe | 38 | 39 | 40 | 41 | 42 | 43 |
| Japan | 38 | 39 | 40 | 41 | 42 | 43 |
| UK | 15 | 15½ | 16 | 16½ | 17 | 17½ |
| USA | 15 | 15½ | 16 | 16½ | 17 | 17½ |

#### Men's Shoes

| Aust/NZ | 7 | 8 | 9 | 10 | 11 | 12 |
|---|---|---|---|---|---|---|
| Europe | 41 | 42 | 43 | 44½ | 46 | 47 |
| Japan | 26 | 27 | 27.5 | 28 | 29 | 30 |
| UK | 7 | 8 | 9 | 10 | 11 | 12 |
| USA | 7½ | 8½ | 9½ | 10½ | 11½ | 12½ |

## Weights & Measures

### Weight
1kg = 2.2lb
1lb = 0.45kg
1g = 0.04oz
1oz = 28g

### Volume
1 litre = 0.26 US gallons
1 US gallon = 3.8 litres
1 litre = 0.22 imperial gallons
1 imperial gallon = 4.55 litres

### Length & Distance
1 inch = 2.54cm
1cm = 0.39 inches
1m = 3.3ft = 1.1yds
1ft = 0.3m
1km = 0.62 miles
1 mile = 1.6km

# lonely planet

Lonely Planet is the world's most successful independent travel information company with offices in Australia, the US, UK and France. With a reputation for comprehensive, reliable travel information, Lonely Planet is a print and electronic publishing leader, with over 650 titles and 22 series catering for travellers' individual needs.

At Lonely Planet we believe that travellers can make a positive contribution to the countries they visit – if they respect their host communities and spend their money wisely. Since 1986 a percentage of the income from books has been donated to aid and human rights projects.

## www.lonelyplanet.com

For news, views and free subscriptions to print and email newsletters, and a full list of LP titles, click on Lonely Planet's award-winning website.

## On the Town

A romantic escape to Paris or a mad shopping dash through New York City, the locals' secret bars or a city's top attractions – whether you have 24 hours to kill or months to explore, Lonely Planet's On the Town products will give you the low-down.

**Condensed guides** are ideal pocket guides for when time is tight. Their quick-view maps, full-colour layout and opinionated reviews help short-term visitors target the top sights and discover the very best eating, shopping and entertainment options a city has to offer.

For more indepth coverage, **City guides** offer insights into a city's character and cultural background as well as providing broad coverage of where to eat, stay and play. **CitySync**, a digital guide for your handheld unit, allows you to reference stacks of opinionated, well-researched travel information. Portable and durable **City Maps** are perfect for locating those back-street bars or hard-to-find local haunts.

*'Ideal for a generation of fast movers.'*

– *Gourmet Traveller* on Condensed guides

## Condensed Guides

- Amsterdam
- Athens
- Bangkok (Oct 2002)
- Barcelona
- Boston
- Chicago
- Dublin
- Frankfurt
- Hong Kong
- London
- Los Angeles (Oct 2002)
- New York City
- Paris
- Prague
- Rome
- San Francisco (Oct 2002)
- Singapore (Oct 2002)
- Sydney
- Tokyo
- Venice (June 2002)
- Washington, DC

# index

*See also separate indexes for Places to Eat (p. 126), Places to Stay (p. 127), Shops (p. 127) and Sights with map references (p. 128).*

## PLACES TO EAT